Failure
is never
Final

Failure
is never
Final

The story of
Janny van der Klis

Told by
Lynda Neilands

Christian Focus

ISBN 185 792 575 0

Revised and expanded edition published in 2000
by Christian Focus Publications, Geanies House,
Fearn, Ross-shire, IV20 1TW, Great Britain.

Previously published in 1994 by Marshall Pickering.

Cover design by Owen Daily.

Contents

Foreword

It is a great joy to write a few words to make Janny's life a best-seller. No, I don't mean this book! Naturally I hope its challenging message will be read by many. But it is her life I am talking about.

Paul said our lives are like letters. The Bible is not written for unbelievers: we should read and believe it, but our lives are the messages that can move unbelievers to turn to God's Book.

You see, all the stories about men and women in the Bible, with the beautiful climax in Hebrews 11, are about ordinary people, who did by faith things which, without faith, they could never have done. Hebrews 11 is also the only chapter which is unfinished; God writes a few more verses every day – about ordinary people who realize their own weakness, but when confronted with need (in this world so full of need) rise to the occasion and let him take over.

Once during the devotional hour at my Missionary Training College in Glasgow the study director spoke about Romans 8:32. 'He who did not spare his own Son, but gave him up for us all – how will he not also, along with him, graciously give us all things?' After reading that verse the director paused. Then he said something which was a divine revelation to me – and one from which I continue to draw daily. 'If you look around and see anything in another person that you would like your life to be enriched with, you can ask God to give it to you on the basis of 'he that spared not his own Son, shall he not also give....'

As I said, to me this was a divine revelation. But when I went to see the director and thank him for that great encouragement, with an almost worried look on his face, he said: 'Andrew, if only you knew, I am constantly scraping the bottom.'

'Constantly scraping the bottom.' Maybe you know that feeling – of total inadequacy, of hopelessness, of unworthiness, of wondering why God ever called you. In this book Janny reveals that she knows the feeling too. But she also shares a secret that many other ordinary people have discovered. The bottom is actually the top of God's endless resources.

This is Janny's experience all right.

It can be yours.

And mine.

And all this by faith as we follow him in obedience to the great commission and the great commandment.

To God be the glory!

Brother Andrew

Prologue

It was 10:15 a.m. on Monday 6th September. My knees shook as I walked towards the lectern. My stomach was in a knot. There they sat behind their desks. Rows of women from all denominations. Young faces. Older faces. Strong faces. Anxious faces. Faces marked by the many problems and often unspoken burdens ordinary women bear. How would they respond to this – my first ever lecture?

It wasn't that I was unused to public speaking. In the past I had enjoyed my spells of deputation, travelling from church to church talking about my missionary work. But those days of deputation were over. And this was the new 'me' – standing with a handful of oh-so-painstakingly-prepared lecture notes – about to launch out into uncharted territory....

I was aware of forty-odd sets of eyes viewing me warily – much as I had viewed my own lecturers in my college days. As a person of authority, wisdom, experience – uttering words to be recorded and remembered – a setter and marker of essays – one who could build up or shatter their fragile self-esteem?

If only they knew!

My own self-esteem was as fragile as a recently mended vase.

The cracks had been appearing for years. But a turn of events less than ten months previously had caused the final smash. Normally I am self-controlled, not given to emotional outbursts of any kind, but one afternoon despair had stripped me of my defences. 'I'm on the scrap-heap!' I had wept, without caring who saw or heard.

That period of total darkness and helplessness lasted for several days. Then fragment by fragment, my life had come back together again. I began to see that I had a future after all. No, not the one I had battled for. Nor the one I had believed and hoped for in its place. But one which my heavenly Father in his all-knowing wisdom had seen fit to provide.

Tentatively, apprehensively, with the cracks still showing, I had come to work in Belfast Bible College. Now, three months later, I had reached this milestone. I stood before the members of the Women's Study Fellowship.

I dared to hope that I might be used by God. Only a few weeks previously a couple of phrases from the story of the feeding of the five thousand as recorded in John's Gospel had struck me afresh. 'Gather the pieces left over; let us not waste any,' Jesus had told his disciples after everyone had eaten their fill.

'The pieces left over' for me were not scraps of bread and fish. They were the lessons learnt over the last thirty years, almost twenty of which I had spent on the mission field. 'Gather them up....let us not waste any,' I seemed to hear the Lord say.

I lifted the first page of my lecture notes. 'Good morning, everyone.' My voice sounded a great deal more confident than I felt. 'As you probably know my name is Janny van der Klis....'

I saw their expectant faces. Oh how I identified with them – with their needs, their hopes, their fears. Many, I already knew, were coping with circumstances much more difficult than my own....

So I stood at the lectern. One part of the story I'm about to relate formed the backdrop to my lectures, slipping out – a detail here, another there – by way of illustration. The other part unfolded as together we studied and shared.

Those women had come seeking God's perspective on their lives. I too was a learner, seeking his perspective on my own immediate past.

This then is the record of lessons to date....

1

Not Just The Wrapper

I had only the vaguest notion of what missionaries did. All I knew was that I wanted to be one. For several years I had been searching, trying to find the living heart of the faith I had grown up with; some core of spiritual reality amidst the rules which had always governed my behaviour. Finally, over a period of days – amazing life-transforming days – I discovered the joy of relationship with God. It was like being lifted out of a mucky goldfish bowl into a sparkling clear ocean. I had the freedom to swim further than I had ever dreamed possible. For with that relationship came a new direction in life; a deep inner conviction that I should bring the message of God's love to people who had never heard it before.

I was a shy girl, reserved to the point of awkwardness, but somehow the youth leader responsible for the group of which I was part seemed to have insight into my feelings. He handed me a list of names and addresses. 'Bible Colleges,' he explained. 'Something you might like to consider.'

I considered for all of two seconds! And my decision was made.

I was a Christian. I had been called into mission. Bible College was a must!

But how was I going to break the news to my parents?

My father and mother were pillars of the church community in the small Dutch town where we lived. They were Reformed and proud of it. We hadn't much money, but they had taught us to see we possessed something of far greater value than silver and gold. A theology. Values. A moral code. I had grown up with a strong sense of spiritual superiority. We were right. The rest of the world, no matter how well-meaning, was sadly in error. But now, at twenty years of age – an age when, in my parents' eyes, I ought to be finding a suitable husband and establishing a Reformed home of my own – it seemed I was falling into error myself. Encountering God outside the tight fabric of my tradition.

While singing choruses round the campfire against a backdrop of glorious Austrian scenery this hadn't seemed to matter. As I travelled back to Holland though, I knew my newfound personal faith was about to be put to the test.

'Lord, please help me,' I prayed by my bed that night. I had already decided to visit home the following day. I knew the longer I put off the inevitable confrontation, the harder it would be.

My parents lived in Oudewater – a town steeped in history: birthplace of the theologian, Arminius; besieged by the Spaniards in the sixteenth century. I had a bedsit in nearby Utrecht. As always the twenty kilometre bus-journey home seemed to take forever. But this time I didn't mind. I savoured the unchallenging peace of the countryside – the green fields dotted with black and white Friesian cattle, the blue-grey glint of the canals, the sharp points of the church spires in the surrounding towns and villages....De Meern....Montfoort.

The bus stopped on the outskirts of my home town.

I had walked its narrow streets between their gabled 16th and 17th century houses so often, I could have made my way home with my eyes shut: past the huge imposing 'Hervormde' church – along the side of the canal – down a couple of side streets. Within a few minutes I had reached a small house opposite the less imposing, but no less influential 'Gereformeerde' church my family attended. My father was the church caretaker – another fact which bound him to the building and all it stood for, body and soul.

With quickening pulse I pushed open the door.

'Mum, Dad, I'm back!'

I was ushered inside – into the cosy back kitchen with its glowing stove.

Once there I let my defences slip for a while, simply enjoying our Saturday evening routine. It was all exactly as usual. My sister Anneke and I helped Mum prepare a simple meal: bread, cold meats, cheese. We ate. Then Dad took the Bible from the shelf and, according to his custom (he'd done it after every meal for as long as I could remember), read a chapter aloud. The table was cleared. The dishes washed. The chairs pushed back.

'Now Janny,' Mum handed round steaming cups of freshly made coffee, her dark eyes sparkling with expectation. 'We want to hear all about your trip.'

'That's right.' My father nodded agreement.

This was it. The moment had come!

It would have been so easy to give them an edited version of what had happened, focusing on those aspects of my experience with which they could identify. They already knew I'd gone to Austria with a group of young people from Youth for Christ to help in a refugee camp. Like many Dutch people my parents had a strong social conscience. They would have viewed a holiday spent helping refugees in an entirely favourable light.

Concern and sympathy were written all over my mother's face as I began to describe the situation. The refugees in question had come from the Eastern block countries. Many had been

16

forced to leave their homes and belongings. For the young and fit the refugee camps had provided temporary shelter before they went on to rebuild their lives elsewhere. But for the old and vulnerable there was no 'elsewhere' – for over a decade those Austrian camps had been their only home.

An ancient castle had housed the refugees I'd visited – spacious living-quarters certainly, but also very damp and draughty! I described the rows of beds in cavernous high-ceilinged rooms, the people sitting on them day after day, locked in hopelessness. Even my father's stern face softened at the thought.

But there was more – so much more.

I talked of Adrie and Gre, the two Dutch girls our group had gone to assist.

'They work as missionaries,' I explained. 'Living in a caravan near the castle.'

Even as I spoke, the memories came flooding back – of those two women, not much older than myself – of the way they'd prayed, and the way God had answered their prayers – of the love I'd seen them pour out day after day. I'd watched them literally washing feet. I'd seen smiles crack wrinkled refugee faces, seen expressions changed from despair to hope at their words.

'Jesus was there. He was in them, working through them.'

My tone was intense, but not half as intense

as my longing that I might convey the essence of what I had experienced. Jesus! A living active Saviour, making his home in human flesh. Filling ordinary folk with his love. Making them missionaries – able to share that love with others.

'I...I want to be like that,' I blurted, finally reaching the crunch. 'Whilst I was there, the Lord became so real to me. I want to tell others. I was thinking of going to Bible College.'

'Bible College,' Mum repeated faintly.

My father said nothing at all.

His face had the hard closed look I had seen so often over the years. I stammered out what little I knew of Bible College, doing my best to make it appear an acceptable option. But I might as well have tried to justify a decision to dye my hair green.

He didn't speak another word to me for the rest of the evening.

I returned to Utrecht with a sense of sober satisfaction. Despite the unpleasantness, I felt I had taken a small but significant step in the right direction.

The logical thing to do next was to find a Bible College to go to.

At that stage I could have written what I knew about such establishments on the back of a very thin bookmark and still have left room for a text! All I could do was study the list the youth leader had given me. Most colleges seemed to be offering three-year courses. Three whole years! Was there nowhere that could programme an aspiring missionary more quickly? Yes. Swansea Bible College, I noted, had cut the time by one third.

But would the authorities even consider taking me in? Painstakingly – since the letter had to be in English – I wrote to inquire. A few weeks later I had my reply. 'Are you sure that's what it says?' Scarcely daring to believe I checked and rechecked the translation. And yes, it seemed there was no mistake. A place had been reserved for me in the Bible College of Wales for the new term, starting in October.

Again I went to see my parents. Again I felt the weight of their disapproval and more than that – the burden of their disgrace. It was like an adult version of the time my brother Jan had dropped a marble in church. Only this time I was the glass ball rolling down the aisle in public view, drawing attention of the pursed-lip, raised eyebrow sort to our family pew. What would the Minister think? Worse still, what might he say?

My father asked to see a copy of the College's statement of faith.

He couldn't find fault with the translation, but he was clearly far from happy. Still he didn't forbid me to go – that had never been his way. He believed in giving everyone, including his eldest daughter, enough rope to hang themselves.

I was told that on no account should I ever come to him looking for money!

It was hard living with his displeasure. My natural desire is to fit in – to please those in authority, and my father's good opinion had always been important to me. The fact that I had only the haziest notion of what going to Bible College would entail didn't help. I saw it as a gateway – a necessary gateway which I must pass through if I was to become what God wanted me to be and serve as he intended me to serve in the future. Still I could see logic in some of my father's arguments: there was, after all, plenty of opportunity for me to get involved in church organisations at home.

So why did I feel so strongly that God had plans for me overseas? Could I be mistaken in my sense of call? What had happened to me in Austria? I had found a new spiritual reality in relationship with Christ, of that I was sure. But was the rest mere emotion? The product of too many choruses and not enough sleep? Perhaps there was no need for all this family tension. Perhaps I could please my heavenly Father and my human father at the same time after all.

During that time of uncertainty I received an invitation to a Christian meeting organized by the Full Gospel Businessmen's Association in

Utrecht. I'd never heard the speaker before –
although rumour had it he was 'interesting' –
something of an oddball as far as the establishment were concerned. 'He's been doing work
behind the iron curtain,' my friend had explained.
More to the point, though Dutch, he'd been to a
British Bible College. Mentally I sized him up
as he made his way to the microphone. Average
height. Brown hair. Reassuringly ordinary. Yet
someone who had done what I was hoping to
do. It seemed such a promising coincidence.
'Lord, please use this man to encourage me,' I
prayed.

I suppose I was thinking of spiritual
encouragement in terms of a comforting warm
bath – soothing away my personal tensions.

What I got was more like an injection of
backbone.

Brother Andrew (for that was the speaker's
name!) began by relating some of his own
experiences. Bang went my impression of
ordinariness! But it was not just the extraordinary
nature of his experiences which held me
spellbound – it was the depth of his commitment.
And if one ordinary person could do extraordinary things because of his extraordinary
commitment to an extraordinary God, why not
others? Why not ME?'

'The servant is not above his master,' Brother
Andrew was saying. 'He was mocked, ridiculed

21

and eventually killed. Are you willing to give your life to God for missionary service? You may receive the same treatment. Service means sacrifice. There is always a way in. There may not be a way out again. Are you willing?'

There were probably around 3,000 people in that auditorium, but every sentence he spoke seemed directed at me.

At the end of his message I rose, eyes closed. Tears were streaming down my face; tears not of sadness, but of deep love and joy. 'Yes, Lord,' I answered, 'I am willing. I'll go wherever you want, whatever the cost.'

Back in my comfortable bedsit the emotion surrounding this response faded, but not its effect on my will. I saw that God's word exhorted me to love him above anyone or anything else – father, mother, brothers, sisters, houses, lands.

I gave in notice at my place of work. My colleagues, who were nearly all churchgoers, were not slow to express their opinions. Going to Bible College!! Had I thought of the consequences? What would I live on? Was it not rash to throw away a promising career?

I did not have any answer to these questions, any more than I had answers to my parents'. What I did have by this stage, was a deep assurance that I was not acting upon some fanciful whim, but in obedience to a genuine call of God.

I left Holland on a murky October evening in 1959.

My parents came with me to the Hook to see me off. How can I convey the pain of our parting? Perhaps the closest analogy is with the feelings of parents who watch their children emigrate. These days my journey across that stretch of water to England would scarcely call for more than a hug and a handshake. Businessmen jet over for breakfast and can be back home for tea. For me, though, there was no comforting vision of imminent homecoming. I had a single ticket in my pocket and no return fare. As far as Mum and Dad were concerned, I might as well have been setting sail for the other side of the world.

'Take care, dear.' Mum's face was stricken as she kissed me goodbye.

My father, as usual, displayed little emotion. But he was there, despite his strong objections – and that said it all.

I stood on deck watching and waving until their dear familiar figures grew small and finally vanished into the night. Would I ever see them again? I felt a wave of desolation. And as I stood there some words I'd heard as a child came back to me.

It had been the custom for my school to raise money every year to support missionaries in Indonesia. On one occasion our project had involved collecting stamps and silver paper. I had worked with enthusiasm, soaking stamps off letters and saving the silver-paper wrapper of the chocolate bar which was our Sunday treat. My contribution to the mission-field had grown rapidly and I was rather proud of my box of stamps and the neat little pile of silver-paper which I carried to school one Monday morning. It felt good to be doing something for people in other lands. I was also looking forward to the reaction of my form-teacher – a kind, older man whom I liked very much.

I caught sight of him crossing the playground and skipped over to hand in my parcel.

As he accepted it, he looked at the silver-paper and then, with his kind eyes resting on me, said: 'That's lovely, my dear. You have worked very hard. Shall I tell you a secret, though? If you really want to give to the missionfield, you should not just give the silver wrapper, but also the chocolate inside.'

Now, years later, as I stood on the deck of that ship on that damp starless night I knew I was entering into the meaning of those words. What God required was the gift of myself – not just my time or my efforts or my money. I lingered a little longer, then went below to my berth....

'Miss van der Klis?' the purser frowned. 'You ought to have been here earlier. I'm afraid your cabin has been taken.'

I couldn't help but smile. Brother Andrew had asked if I was willing to face torture, even martyrdom for the sake of Christ. Now I recognized that the path of self-sacrifice was often of a much less dramatic nature.

What lay on the other side of the Channel I could not tell.

My great adventure began with a stuffy sleepless night spent seated on my suitcase.

2

Jehovah Jireh

'That is Glynderwen,' my guide pointed up towards a stately mansion overlooking Mumbles Bay. 'But you'll be staying with the other girls in Derwen Fawr.' We drove a little farther along the road and there it was – another stately mansion, equally imposing. Once those neighbouring estates had hosted the great and wealthy of the land. Now they were home to Swansea Bible College.

I was travelling with Dr. Joan, the Dean of Students. Her little black Hillman had come to pick me up at the station. What she made of the tall travel-weary student she found awaiting her, bemused and speechless, I do not know. For my own part – in so far as I was capable of assessing anything – I saw in this stranger everything I aspired to be. Never mind that I could only understand one quarter of what she was saying; she was beautifully turned out in a smart black polka-dot dress, and her eyes conveyed depths of warmth, wisdom and serenity which I longed to possess.

There was a cup of tea and biscuits in her

office when we arrived. But thankfully no official forms. All that could wait until later, she indicated. No doubt those wise eyes had judged I needed time to recover before confronting another major hurdle. A few moments later I found myself upstairs in a six-bedded dormitory alone with my suitcase and my confusion.

As I gazed out of the curved window, taking in the graceful sweep of the gardens, the glorious autumnal colours of the woodland and the glint of sea beyond, an object in the foreground caught my attention. It was a large stone pedestal about four feet in height. Narrowing my eyes, I could just make out two words carved in the stone – Jehovah Jireh.

I did not realize it, but I was studying one of the college's founding principles. The story goes, when Rees Howells set out to find a suitable site for the college, he and his wife had sixteen shillings between them. Two years later they bought the first estate, Glynderwen, at a cost of over $6,000. The purchase of Derwen Fawr swiftly followed, again defying the normal law of economics. Hence the inscription on the pedestal. Jehovah Jireh – the Lord will provide.

As I sat on my bed that afternoon, however, I was unfamiliar with that piece of history. What would my father make of those words, I wondered? I could almost see him shaking his head and telling me, in the voice of one who has just been confirmed in his worst suspicions, that it was no Christian Bible College I'd come to, but the headquarters of some weird sect.

The arrival of my five roommates created a timely diversion, dispelling introspection in a clamour of friendly greetings. Despite the communication problems, I sensed a oneness – some root of common experience – which did much to reassure me. Some of my earlier spiritual certainty began to reassert itself. A bell was sounding somewhere in the depths of the building. I felt a tiny shoot of joyful expectation. So this was Bible College. I'd finally made it. All was about to be revealed....

And what a revelation it was! In those first three months I found myself studying two languages. The first was English – which I learnt amazingly quickly, worrying the dictionary like a frenzied terrier in an effort to get vocabulary off its pages and into my head. The second language might best be described as Evangelical Esperanto; those phrases that are bandied about in Bible Colleges and Christian fellowships, some lifted directly from Scripture, others used to describe common spiritual attitudes and experiences. Getting to grips with Evangelical Esperanto took longer. The dictionary wasn't much help. No amount of leafing through its pages was going to explain the experience of the fellow student who confided that during her 'quiet time' she had had a deep 'inner witness' that she was 'covered by the blood'!

No doubt it would have been good for the Christians who used such cliches to have been challenged to explain exactly what they meant. I didn't have the confidence to do that. Yet, little by little, as the weeks went by, I had the thrill of seeing the Holy Spirit reveal the fragrant truths and experiences that underlay this evangelical code.

One example stands out in my memory. Some months after my arrival the post brought a letter from my brother Jan. The moment I read it I knew my future hung in the balance. There were problems at home, he told me. Major problems. My mother had had a nervous breakdown. There was talk of taking her into hospital.

What should I do? Mum and I had always been very close. Of all the family, I was the one she had tended to confide in. My brother didn't say it openly, but I could read between the lines. He was telling me I should return home immediately. My mother's health was at stake.

The obvious person to talk to under the circumstances was Dr. Joan. As Dean of Students, she had pastoral responsibility for all the girls – but even if she hadn't had the official title, I should have been drawn to seek her out anyway, as a person of maturity, wisdom and faith.

I was not in any way disappointed with the way she received me. Indeed no one could have asked for a more sympathetic listening ear. But her final words only served to worsen my confusion.

'Janny, dear,' she said gently as we parted. 'This is a very tricky problem. I believe you should go back to your room and seek a word from the Lord.'

As usual I was far too shy and reserved to admit I hadn't a clue what she meant. Instead I went back to my room just as advised, and tore my hair in desperation.

'Lord,' I said, 'I've been told to seek a word from you. But I don't know what that means or how to do it.'

And then I noticed that my Bible was open on the bed. I picked it up and found myself reading a verse from Psalm 34: 'Many are the afflictions of the righteous, but the LORD delivers him out of them all' (verse 19).

I experienced a wave of relief. If there had been another letter from Jan pushed under the door, entirely negating the first, I couldn't have felt a stronger reassurance.

God was telling me that I didn't have to do anything – that he personally would deliver me and my mother from this problem.

And putting two and two together, if the Lord had spoken to me through his word, the Bible, it meant I could go back to Dr. Joan's office and tell her I'd followed her advice to the letter. I'd sought and received a word from the Lord.

My mother recovered fully. And I remained where I was, continuing on my inner journey of challenge and discovery. Swansea Bible College, I now knew, was about lectures (Old Testament studies, New Testament studies, Church history, Christian ethics, Doctrine). It was about developing practical skills and medical know-how. Above all it was about spiritual growth.

Rees Howells, its founder, had had a very distinctive spiritual formation. Of course the spiritual principles he lived out weren't new. Jesus taught them: the principle of dying to the flesh in order to live by faith; the principle of trusting God to provide for material needs; the principle of obeying the voice of the Spirit rather than the voice of the world. And now I had my opportunity – an opportunity I could never have had in quite the same way in Holland – to try these principles out for myself.

I had drawn out my life savings before leaving home – £35. Enough to cover a single term's fees.

The day I paid for that first term, it seemed only right to mention, rather shamefacedly, to the college Secretary that I had no guarantee that I would be able to pay for the rest of the year.

Her reaction amazed me. 'That's wonderful,' she beamed. 'Now you have the opportunity to trust God.'

I hastily rearranged my face from apologetic to pleased. But my natural caution reasserted itself as I left the office. Dare I believe what I was hearing; that the almighty God, creator of the heavens and the earth, would actually take a personal interest in my college fees?

A few weeks later I found a pound note on the corner of my bed. Nobody in the dormitory knew anything about it. To this day, I still don't know where it came from. But having ascertained that it was definitely meant for me, I danced up the stairs to the office. 'Please put that to my fees,' I told the Secretary. As I saw her take out the huge ledger and mark in the entry, I thought I would explode with wonder and joy. It seemed the principle was working. Even if it meant making money drop from the ceiling, God could supply my needs.

And he did. Throughout the years I spent in Swansea, my needs were always covered. I had sufficient to live on and enough to travel home on holiday each year.

Lest this sounds too glib to be realistic, I might add that I did have some experiences where miraculous deliverance didn't happen. I well remember three of us students working in Cornwall and learning, as Paul puts it 'how to suffer want' as we made one tin of spam last us two days. Such incidents served to remind me that the words 'the Lord will provide' are found at the end of a story geared to take the glib edge off any prosperity teaching. They come from Genesis 22 – the chapter where Abraham travels to the very extremity of faith – to the moment when he lifts the knife to sacrifice his only son and God intervenes, providing a lamb to be sacrificed in Isaac's stead.

'Jehovah Jireh', Abraham names the place where the miracle happens. No grounds for complacency here. No excuse for taking financial responsibilities lightly. No promise of a cushion from every potential hardship. 'Jehovah Jireh' – an assertion, rather, that keeps company with a willingness to sacrifice and a readiness to obey God no matter what......

I had imagined that leaving home and family was the hardest thing I could ever be called to do – and that, having proved myself willing for such a sacrifice, the path of obedience would be relatively straightforward from then on. Within a few months of my arrival at Derwen Fawr I was to discover that this was far from being the case. I had no difficulty outwardly conforming to the requisite standards of Christian behaviour. As far as the rules were concerned I was a model student. But shortly after my arrival something happened to make me realize that there was still

33

plenty of room for rebellion in my heart.

It began when I was made responsible for sweeping and polishing the spacious entrance hall every morning. This in itself was no problem. I understood that the Bible College budget did not allow for the payment of any domestic staff and that household duties should be part of our training. Cleanliness in any case had always been next to godliness in my book. I was determined to be as faithful in my brushing and polishing as in Bible Study and prayer....

The problem arose because I was supposed to share the workload with a fellow student. But within a few days it became clear that the scriptural principle involved hadn't made much impact on Jenny. There I would be on my hands and knees polishing the parquet floor for all I was worth, and she would finally emerge wiping the sleep from her eyes, just in time to pick up my cloths and brushes before breakfast.

Not fair. Lazy. Unspiritual. Self-indulgent. Taking advantage....Those were the sort of thoughts that filled my mind as I greeted her each morning.

And those were the sort of thoughts on which God put his finger when I knelt before him in prayer.

'Yes, I want you to continue to do the work to the best of your ability, but I also want you to stop judging Jenny,' he seemed to say.

What a small request! But what a battle! To obey meant letting go of my right to be irritated and annoyed. It meant reaching that place where I could turn from my polishing, smile and say 'Good morning, Jenny,' and really mean it. No pointed looks. No gritted teeth. No undercurrents.

'You will meet other Jennys on the mission field,' the Lord pointed out. 'The world is full of them. This is your opportunity to learn how to react.'

So I learnt. Slowly. Painfully. Some sacrifices can be made once and for all but this was a daily inner struggle. Sometimes I felt I was making progress. Other times I felt the irritation rise in my throat. But by the time I was assigned a new set of duties in the kitchen, there existed between Jenny and myself a peaceable working relationship (I can't even remember whether she began pulling her weight or not – which shows how little it mattered really!). Even more important there was a strong bond of sisterly love.

One battle ends and another begins! A whole year had passed and it was time for a trip home to Holland. Much as I longed to see my parents, I was anticipating conflict. My study and reading of the Bible had brought a call to a further outward step of obedience – that of water baptism. I had a strong suspicion this wouldn't go down well with my father.

I was right. Never in all my life had I seen

Dad as angry as he was when I told him of my intention. He was literally white with rage. Through clenched lips he informed me that I was bringing disgrace on the entire family.

'Daddy,' I protested, 'If I were drunk and lying in some gutter you would have justification for saying that.'

Actually a drunken daughter might have been easier for him to bear. It would have been less of a threat than this daughter who seemed bent on flinging the theological framework of her whole upbringing back in his face; challenging not only his righteousness, but that of the Christian community of which he was part.

The path of obedience that summer was a lonely, soul-searing experience. Dad's sense of communal outrage was no figment of his imagination. To avoid the horror of being 'read out' of the church, I decided to withdraw my membership voluntarily. Where once I had been known and accepted, I was now an outcast. I saw former friends and neighbours turn their backs on me in the street. It hurt. Of course it did. But as many who have undergone similar experiences would testify, there was blessing in the pain. 'I will purify you just as metal is refined and will remove all your impurity,' I read in Isaiah (1:25). I returned to Bible College that October with a deep awareness of God's loving refining hand upon my life.

It came as something of a shock to discover that I was now one of the more senior students. For so long I had seen myself as a spiritual and linguistic greenhorn struggling to make the grade. Now there was a new batch of first years, many of whom knew less than I did. Still nothing could have prepared me for the letter I received towards the end of that year.

It was from Dr. Joan.

Apparently she felt I should become head of the girl students the following term.

Head student! To me this was the spiritual equivalent of a worm being asked to become king of the jungle. As head student I would be expected to address the other girls regularly. Inarticulate and reserved as I still was, this seemed totally beyond me. I couldn't even manage to read the Bible aloud in class without choking on the words. Yet the very unexpectedness of the request bore the stamp of the Spirit. I knew my deep sense of inadequacy could be no excuse for turning it down. So, in fear and trembling, I accepted.

At this time I was in the habit of visiting a young couple who lived close to the college. Valerie and Len were their names. They took a great interest in us college students and regularly invited us into their home. I loved to go there – and not just because their cosy sitting-room made a welcome change from the vast expanses of Derwen Fawr. There was a freshness about their Christianity – a vitality and lack of pretence which I found particularly attractive.

And then, one Sunday, I arrived to find another visitor in the sitting-room – a diminutive lady with a bun and a little hat perched on her head who was introduced to me as Valerie's Auntie Jeannie.

Despite her traditional appearance it didn't take me long to work out that Auntie Jeannie was not the sort of little old lady given to sitting quietly in the corner with her knitting. She looked me straight in the eye.

'Are you going to the mission field?' she inquired.

I admitted that yes that was indeed what I hoped to do.

'Are you baptised in the Holy Ghost?' came the next question – again accompanied by that gentle searching gaze.

It was like being back in Dr. Joan's office wondering where on earth I should begin to seek a word from the Lord. 'Umm....I don't know....' I hesitated.

'Well you'd better not go without being sure, dear,' said this epitome of matter-of-fact spirituality. 'Would you like me to pray for you?'

With my deep sense of need, I was not going to turn down any opportunity of being prayed for.

'Oh yes please,' I agreed eagerly.

I have never taken up any strong theological position on baptism in the Spirit. I can only speak of what happened to me – and of the subsequent effects of that experience on my life.

Shortly after Auntie Jeannie began to pray, the presence of God became more real to me even than at the time of my conversion. First I saw into my own heart. Up until that moment I had never come under a deep conviction of sin. I had, after all, led an outwardly blameless life by human standards. But now those standards were wiped away, and what I saw horrified me. The petty-mindedness. The pride. The self-seeking. I wept and wept.

And then, just as clearly, the Father showed me his Son. I saw him hanging on the cross – bearing my sin – getting rid of it once and for all through the outpouring of his blood.

My tears stopped. Joy flooded my being and I found myself praising God aloud. It was as if a passage had been opened between my voice and my spirit. Words were flowing from me – neither Dutch nor English. I was speaking in a language I'd never used before.

In the end Auntie Jeannie and Valerie left me to it. I'm not sure how much time elapsed before I came back down to earth – maybe an hour, maybe two. But I brought a bit of heaven with me. In the weeks that followed I noted a number of changes in my life. Where once I had been in the habit of waking at nights in a cold sweat, haunted by nightmares, now I woke up almost choking with joy. I retained the ability to speak in tongues. Most significantly, I lost my painful shyness. The thought of speaking publicly no longer knotted my stomach. I had a new confidence, a sort of spiritual boldness, together with a new flow of English words. It seemed that having allowed my name to go forward for the position of head girl, I had seen God's ability to equip me for the task.

That equipping couldn't have been more timely. Shortly after I became head student Dr. Joan took ill. Her absence created a huge pastoral gap in the life of the college. During the months which followed I began to discover what it was like to exercise authority – to be the one to whom the other girls looked for encouragement. There is nothing like having to strengthen the faith of others to drive one deeper into the Word of God. Now, as I sat with my Bible, I wasn't just trying to discern what he was saying to me as an individual, but what he was saying to a group of well over twenty girls.

I remember on one occasion being particularly burdened by the struggles many were having to find their fees for that particular term. I knelt for hours before the Lord seeking that position of faith where I knew he was able not only to supply my own needs but everyone else's as well. Finally I went to speak to the students. I shared with them the familiar verse from Luke's gospel: 'Follow me and I will make you fishers of men' (Matt. 4:19).

'We aren't just here to learn,' I elaborated. 'We are here to be made effective in God's service. And part of the process through which he makes us is by allowing needs to come into our lives. When we lack something, it isn't because he delights in causing us hardship, but in order that we may prove him. Because what we prove him to be becomes part of us. It is more than knowledge – it is his very life taking deeper possession of our hearts.'

In the prayer-time which followed I knew that message had struck home. Gone was the oppressive burden of need. There was a fresh vision of God. There was worship. There was praise. And the post next morning brought concrete proof of the breakthrough. Many of those girls received letters with gifts to meet their material needs.

On one level this was all very positive, confirming that I had been 'fitted' to my position. Yet by the end of that final year I was once again in inner turmoil.

Africa beckoned. I wanted to do nothing more than to apply for missionary service. Why was it then, that at the very moment when the end of all this training was in sight, I had no peace about taking the necessary steps to fulfil my dearest ambition?

I argued with God. It didn't make sense. There were thousands of Christians committed to staying at home – only a tiny percentage willing to go overseas.

Then one night as I was on my knees pleading yet again for permission to go to Africa, God showed me something. Almost as in a vision he portrayed before my eyes a map of the world without any frontiers or boundaries. And while I looked at this map, he spoke to me and said: 'The field is the world and it does not matter where you are as long as you are in my will.'

The next morning I went to the college authorities and told them of my feelings. I asked whether it would be possible for me to stay on in the college as a member of staff. I was willing to work in the kitchens or the laundry – wherever.

In fact they already had a very specific job in mind. My offer had coincided with the news that Dr. Joan's condition was even more serious than had first been thought. With no prospect of her return to Derwen Fawr in the foreseeable future, my request, they said, was an answer to prayer.

As I realized what God was doing I experienced an incredible joy and peace. Once again, it seemed, the college's founding principle had held firm. Jehovah Jireh – the Lord will provide. Only now I knew what it was like to be on the delivering rather than the receiving end of that provision!

3

Shattered Illusions

I remained at Swansea Bible College for a further four years, right into the middle of the sixties. While young people in the outside world swung to the music of the Beatles and put flowers in their hair, I kept my skirts at a modest length and attended staff meetings, taking responsibility for a range of pastoral and domestic matters in Derwen Fawr. I soon found it hard to remember any other way of life. And indeed my annual trips home to Holland revealed just how rapidly past ways were being eroded. The church community had shrunk. Its influence no longer permeated our neighbourhood to the same degree. Even the minister seemed smaller somehow – and certainly less formidable.

One positive outcome, as far as my relationship with my parents was concerned, was that my deviance from the traditional norm seemed much less offensive. I saw Dad's attitude soften from outrage into a certain grudging respect. Other people's children were dropping out, taking drugs, living with their boyfriends. I, at least, had adopted a Christian lifestyle – and what's more, I wasn't costing him a penny! My brother Jan had gone to theological college. Finding the money for his fees was no small burden. 'It's different with Janny,' Dad was overheard telling a friend, with the faintest hint of pride. 'She just prays and the money comes.'

I was in my late twenties by this stage. Old enough to make a more positive contribution to discussions with senior members of staff, yet still young enough to identify with the students. I continued to model myself on Dr. Joan. I suppose at some level I assumed my life would follow a similar pattern; that I would serve God within the college community until illness or death intervened.

And then with dramatic swiftness a very different future was laid before me.

It all began in the drying-room.

The drying-room, let me explain, was something of a grey area as far as college regulations were concerned. Rule number eight forbade any unnecessary contact between members of the opposite sex. Clearly this meant no chitchat over meals, no fraternizing in the grounds or corridors. The boundaries became somewhat blurred, however, in the steamy atmosphere of the drying-room. There, male and female students might move with impunity from that level of contact essential to determine how much line-space should be allotted to his shirts

45

and how much to her blouses, to matters of a more intimate nature.

And there, one afternoon, a remark was addressed to me which set my whole well-ordered, rule-abiding college existence reeling.

The speaker was a third-year student of the opposite sex.

'I see John Mullen has been paying you a lot of attention lately, Janny,' he remarked.

Almost as a reflex action my mind conjured up a picture of tall dark John Mullen. He was head student that year – in which capacity his path had frequently crossed with mine.

'Has he?' Burying my confusion in a bundle of clean washing I made my escape. But there was no escaping from the consequences of the observation. From that moment I saw John Mullen in a totally new light. And there was no doubt about it, he was paying me a lot of attention. There was definitely something more than respect in the number of times he had held the door open for me; in the way he complimented me on the colour of a dress. He was interested in me as a person. I could sense it now from the other side of a crowded lecture room. What's more – I was beginning to feel the same way.

A smile here, a meeting of eyes there and these feelings were communicated. Before long

John in person appeared at my side in the drying-room. 'We need to meet, Janny. I want to talk to you.'

There was nothing I wanted more myself.

Drastic situations called for drastic measures! Term would be over in a few months' time. John would be leaving the college. As far as getting to know one another was concerned, it was now or never.

We arranged to meet in the wooded area outside Derwen Fawr that evening. It was to be the first of many such meetings. We would stand together amongst the trees and talk and talk – getting to know one another, sharing past experiences, making plans. If I felt a certain amount of guilt at such blatant infringement of rule number eight, I could salve my conscience (not altogether successfully) with the thought that the rule was designed for students, not members of staff.

Notwithstanding my dislike of the secrecy surrounding my romance, I was walking on air, praising God for the wonderful new future which had opened out before me. John and I were thinking in terms of marriage. The plan was that I should leave the college and travel with him to Ireland during the summer to meet his friends and family. I would remain there when he went to Nigeria in the autumn. One thing we hadn't quite decided was whether our wedding should take place in Ireland, in Holland or in Africa – the continent of my dreams.

Breaking the news of my imminent departure to the Bible College staff was hard. But they were very understanding. They even took on board my reservations about rule number eight. The restraints it imposed were unrealistic, I argued. Marriage was part of God's plan for creation, after all. And you might as well try to stop the earth spinning on its axis, as try to prevent young people from falling in love. Surely a better policy would be to recognize and accommodate this – officially permitting such couples to spend time together.

There was a lump the size of a small egg in my throat the day John and I stood outside the college for the last time, awaiting the bus that would transport us to the station. Glancing back down that broad sweeping driveway, I realized how much I was leaving behind. Yet I was also bringing so much with me. The spiritual principles taught and practised within those grey stone walls had moulded my life – and I would continue to live by them. In Ireland. In Africa. Wherever.

It was to be a year of partings – first from those dear Christian colleagues, a little later from John himself. Another egg in the throat job that.

'I'll write every week,' I promised, longing for the day when I would be travelling to Nigeria at his side.

But in the meantime there was plenty to keep me busy. As planned I had remained in Northern Ireland. I had a job working with a Christian organisation. I was making friends, and had linked up with a local church fellowship.

It would be nice to say I made an effortless transition from one Christian community to another. The truth of the matter is that for a while I almost lost my spiritual bearings in what I can only call the maze of denominationalism. No matter which way I turned, I seemed to tread on someone's sensibilities. Shortly after I started attending this particular church, I was asked to give my testimony. I welcomed the opportunity but was rather taken aback afterwards to be greeted with pursed-lip disapproval.

'You shouldn't have mentioned Billy Graham,' I was informed.

A few months later I was wrong-footed again when I arrived at the home of a Christian friend joyfully brandishing one of the first modern versions of the Bible. Another major faux pas. The translation was unacceptable. Apparently I must continue my struggle with the beautiful but unpronounceable (for a native Dutch speaker) language of the Authorized Version.

Accordingly I carefully checked the text on the get-well card I bought for a child in my Sunday-school class, making sure it was suitably 'authorized'. But still my reward was a click of

49

the tongue and a disapproving shake of the head. No, there was nothing heretical about the card *per se* – it was just that I'd bought it in the wrong Christian bookshop!

It was all very confusing. What puzzled me most was that the very people who seemed so sure of their scriptural ground in these peripheral areas, seemed to take clear biblical injunctions – about pride, backbiting, turning the other cheek, for example – a lot less seriously.

I had always maintained that we can have Christian fellowship with all believers, whatever their individual experience and shades of belief, at the foot of the cross. At Bible College this had worked – with students from many different denominations worshipping and living together in harmony. Yet after struggling for over a year to fit in to my new church fellowship on that basis, I had to admit to a sense of failure and spiritual unreality.

What should I do? Leave that particular church and look for fellowship elsewhere? It seemed churlish and ungrateful when many of the members had gone out of their way to help me practically and make me feel at home. I resolved to grit my teeth and keep trying. After all I wasn't going to be in Northern Ireland for ever. My lacy white wedding dress hung in the wardrobe – the gift of a loving friend. Marriage would solve everything, I expected fondly. All I had to do was fit in for a little longer....

How easy it is to spot areas of unreality in other people's spiritual lives and miss the unreality in our own! John's letter took me completely by surprise. I came down one morning and there it was – a letter in which he expressed his doubts about our relationship, in which he suggested we shouldn't have contact for the next few months, but should separately pray and seek God's will for the future.

To say I was shattered would be an understatement. It was as if one minute I had a part in a drama – a costume, lines, a clear sense of direction. And the next minute someone had turned on the house lights, revealing the whole thing for what it was. Illusion. Make believe. Deep down I knew I had ignored the warning signs. The lengthening gaps between John's letters – the increasingly factual nature of the content. But we had both had our roles to play. I had thought that if I could just keep playing mine, then he would play his, and we would all live happily ever after....

Now suddenly the fairytale was over.

'I can't stay here. I want to go home,' I wept into the arms of the friend whose house I shared.

In a matter of hours the flight was booked and a neighbour drove me to the airport. I cried all the way. 'It'll be all right, you'll see,' the neighbour – a non-Christian – tried to be soothing.

'It won't. I've lost everything.' But even as I wept over the shredding of my illusions, there was something deep down telling me that God still had his hand on my life.

That awareness kept me afloat during the tempestuous summer months when all my natural human feelings – of shock, of rejection, of humiliation, of deep, deep longing to see my fiance again – were at their height and I spent hours weeping in my bedroom, unable to face the outside world. 'If I make my bed in the depths, you are there.' I reminded myself over and over again, making the beautiful words of Psalm 139 my own. They held me steady when John came to Holland that Christmas to see me. There would be no scenes, no pleading, no recriminations, I resolved. I knew our romance – such as it had been – was over and that I had to release him. I saw the relief on his face when I took the initiative saying the words he had been afraid to say. We talked far into the night, the sense of God's presence helping us get our relationship onto a new footing – one of friendship and mutual respect.

'What will you do, Janny?' he asked towards the end of the evening as we sat watching the dying embers of the fire.

Now Psalm 139 was a lifeline pulling me steadily from the sea of my lost future. 'Even there your hand will guide me, your right hand will hold me fast.' I had regained my bearings. No, I wouldn't be staying in Holland as everyone seemed to expect.

'I'll go back to Ireland in the New Year,' I told him.

My Irish friends were delighted. They took my unlooked-for return as a personal compliment .... which in some ways it was. Right from the start I had found the people of Northern Ireland exceptionally kind and warm-hearted. And I loved the way the green hills undulated across the skyline – their ups and downs so different from the flat cycle paths of Holland. But of course there had to be more behind my return than that. The best way I could explain it was as the outward expression of an inner certainty that no mistakes had been made; that leaving Bible College, coming to Belfast, and even my broken engagement were all necessary steps along a path leading to some ultimate me-shaped niche, which only I could fill.

I was offered my old job back – but I knew that wasn't my appointed niche, any more than the job I'd been offered in Holland. And in any case my former place of employment seemed one of those areas with which, for emotional reasons as much as anything else, I had to make a clean break. The church also fell into that category. I felt free now to seek out a new place of worship, knowing that such a course of action, under the circumstances, would be generally respected and understood.

So began a long and happy association with Great Victoria Street Baptist Church. The pastor and his wife had served in a church in Weston-super-Mare when I had been in Swansea so I already knew them slightly. Their caring prayer support saw me safely through the potential traumas of giving back my engagement-ring and disposing of the wedding dress.

It became even more vital when a temporary job representing the Africa Inland Mission brought me into contact with senior staff members, all of whom encouraged me to offer for full-time service.

My own prayer-life became punctuated with exclamation marks!

'I can't believe it, Lord!'

'I'm almost afraid to pinch myself in case I wake up!'

'Africa – at long last!'

'You mean it, don't you Lord? This future is for real!'

I got a green light every time. In as many months as it takes to build your average bungalow, I had been accepted for service with the Africa Inland Mission, demonstrated that I had a reasonable expectation of support and most important of all, discovered my me-shaped niche.

It was when I heard AIM missionary Mary Moss speak about the Turkana region of Kenya, telling of an isolated desert area, of its tall nomadic people, that that particular part of the puzzle softly yet unmistakably clicked into place. The hospital there already had nurses, but the mission station desperately needed someone with administrative skills – and I fitted the bill.

Every year, in the month of October, there was a week-long missionary convention in Belfast. The closing Saturday evening was known as 'candidates night', when the spotlight was on those about to leave for the mission field for the first time.

October 1970 saw me being shown to a seat on the platform.

Those were the days when people flocked to missionary conventions – or perhaps it would be more accurate to say that the evangelical population of Northern Ireland flocked to Christian events in general, and missionary conventions were no exception! One way or another the Wellington Hall that evening was packed out.

How glad I was that custom dictated that those taking their seats should bow their heads in prayer. I can't remember what I prayed – for calmness, probably, and a clear mind.

What I do remember is gathering the courage to open my eyes and confront that vast sea of faces only to find myself gazing at one face way up in the back row of the balcony – the face of my ex-fiance.

The thought struck me – but for him I wouldn't be here. No, it wasn't that I was running away from a broken relationship. If the devil ever tried to plague me with that, I knew I would be able to look back on this moment and send him packing. I was going in response to God's call. Yet I could also see how in his sovereign purposes, God had used that relationship to stir me out of one area of service so that I could be directed into another.

John was married now – he'd found his separate niche. And I was bound for Africa.

Our eyes met across that crowded auditorium.

And in my heart I knew nothing but joy.

4

A Dream Come True

Henry, the visiting psychologist, had been with us for a couple of days. He had come to us at Lokori to do some research. What he was researching I am not sure....but it certainly involved a lot of questions.

With customary courtesy – notwithstanding the fact that he had already put in a ten hour day at the hospital and could expect a few more calls before bedtime – Dick Anderson, our team leader, filled him in on the background details. There were seven missionaries currently on the station: himself and his wife Joan, another missionary couple, two nurses – Mary and Essie, and one administrator – me. Our work included running a twenty-four bed hospital, conducting regular medical safaris into the bush, and engaging in a range of activities of an evangelistic nature in conjunction with the local church.

Henry's questions continued next morning in the living-room of the simple three-bedroom bungalow Mary, Essie and I shared.

'Three women in one house. And you really get on well! I've been watching you – the way you relate. So what's the secret?'

His quest for an explanation was cut short when a care assistant from the hospital arrived on the doorstep and announced that the body had been installed in the back of the Land-Rover.

'Body? What body?' Henry wanted to know.

The body of a Turkana man – the head of a family, I explained. And, since the other women were going to be busy in the hospital, the job of transporting him back to his family for burial in the cattle enclosure had fallen to me.

I rose.

Notebook in hand, psychological nose twitching, Henry elected to come too.

'So how do you feel?' was the next question, as we set off along the bumpy road, under the baking sun.

'What do you mean?' I braked to avoid a stray goat, and waved at the Somali proprietor of one of the little shops on the other side of the dry riverbed.

'Knowing that you have a body in the back of the car?' my interlocutor persisted.

'Well, this may sound crude. But it's one of those things that has to be done.'

'What do you think is going to happen?'

My mind flipped over the possibilities. We certainly weren't going to find people sitting in neat rows inside a church building. The Turkana followed a tribal religion – a mixture of super-stition and animism. They took their economic

58

problems to the emuron – or wise man – who consulted animal intestines to predict the future. Their sicknesses were dealt with (at a price) by local healers, who often inflicted terrible wounds with red-hot stones in their attempts to burn out disease. Death shadowed young and old, pouncing like some insatiable beast to snatch its prey. Today an adult. Tomorrow a child.

Sometimes the people used the ritual of sacrifice after a man's death.

On this occasion, however, when we finally reached our destination, the whole community went berserk. I'd never heard such wailing. It was as if all the pent-up pain of their unequal, never-ending struggle filled the air. As the care assistant and I began to unload the white-sheeted body, men produced ropes and knives. Women threatened to kill their children. I looked around for Henry – but he was nowhere to be seen.

Afterwards, though, when we had somehow managed to calm the crowd sufficiently to conduct a simple service, he emerged from the shelter of a thornbush, and pronounced himself impressed.

I don't know what may be printed in some learned journal somewhere as a result of what he saw – but if nothing else his reaction to some of the things we accepted as a matter of course made me realize afresh just how fast I had adjusted to the requirements of this new way of life.

In colonial times the Turkana region of Kenya had been known as the Northern Frontier District – a sealed-off area which white people could not visit without a permit. There was nothing to be got out of it. Its people were nomads, herding their goats and driving their camels and donkeys throughout the huge arid region in a constant search for grazing and water. And Europeans going in and losing themselves were nothing but a nuisance. Now, of course, there was no such restriction. Less than a year previously, tears had sprung to my eyes as I caught my first glimpse of the North African coast – a blaze of white gold sand and blue sea. Two days later I had stepped off the little Cessna plane that had flown me from Nairobi to this, my ultimate destination.

It had been like stepping into a giant populated hair-dryer with a hot wind blowing day and night. I had read much about Turkana and seen slides taken by missionaries who had been there. Yet books and photos could never convey the intensity of the heat, the dust, the smells, the hordes of flies, the effect of seeing half-naked people living in dome-shaped little huts, their thin bodies often covered with tropical sores. This was a place of extremes. Extreme heat. Extreme poverty. Extreme ignorance of the outside world.

It was also a place where the gospel could be seen to be extremely good news.

Every month our friends in the Mission Aviation Fellowship would send a plane to Lokori (road transport was limited and in many cases virtually impossible) which we would load with medical supplies before setting off on a medical safari which could last anything up to a week. Though modern medicine was still eyed with suspicion, the effects of antibiotics had brought about some wonderful cures and faith in injections was growing fast. The bigger the needle, the better people liked it! So much physical suffering could be simply alleviated – some chloroquin tablets, a few eye-drops.

No sooner had we begun to unpack our medical kit in those remote areas, than a crowd would begin to gather; tall naked men, beaded women, their skins richly decorated with scars. Many had never heard before that God had a Son. They had a straightforward rule of thumb which they applied in such matters. There were good words and bad words. You listened to good words. You did not listen to bad words. Early on they had decided that the words we spoke were 'good'. Physical suffering was only one aspect of their problems. With life and livelihood constantly under threat – from the ever-present drought, from disease, from a raid by the neighbouring Pokot tribe (the Pokot were the arch-enemies of the Turkana), they lived in fear and they knew it.

'Where is the pain? Can you show me where it is?' I remember asking one woman in the course of one such clinic. She vaguely pointed at her stomach.

'Does it hurt very much?' She nodded – her face dark, desolate.

'How many days have you felt this pain?' I probed further.

'Since yesterday,' she replied, 'when the Pokot came.'

'Oh, and what happened yesterday to bring you this pain?'

A sudden desperately anxious look made me aware of a far deeper need than the need for medicine. 'They killed four of my children. I have only one left now. They speared them before my eyes. I want to die now too!'

What could I do? What could I say?

In very simple words, I explained the gospel story, telling of the God who made everybody and everything, the One who lives in heaven, who – like her – had only one Son, one very precious Son.

Something happened as I spoke. That story penetrated the fear and desperation. I actually saw a glimmer of comfort in those saddened eyes. She held my hand tightly and said 'Ejok' – thank you.

I was to see the same look in the eyes of a young girl, a few years later, as she lay in the hospital, her stomach ripped open by a Pokot spear. There was no chance of saving her. All I could do was sit by her bed, hold her hand and tell her of Jesus, the Saviour who loved her enough to die on the cross for her sins. Her grip on my hand became tighter. 'He rose from the dead. He has gone to prepare a place for those who trust him, in heaven.' Too weak to speak, she simply nodded. There was nothing in Turkana tradition to give people hope in the face of death. But in the last few minutes of her life, I will always believe I saw that child come to faith.

At home in Europe it was so easy for people to bury their spiritual needs in a wealth of material and mental distractions. The gospel could be neatly compartmentalized. 'I already know all about it – and it has no relevance to me', was the unarticulated reflex response of so many. In this place of extremities, however, the relevance of the spiritual to the natural was never in question.

And often we saw it demonstrated in the most dramatic ways.

Akai was a beautiful Turkana girl in her early twenties. Her problem, according to the tribal elders, was that she had refused to marry an older man who had proceeded to curse her. 'See what you can do and if you can't do anything we'll take her back,' they said with an air of resignation.

Their words confirmed our own suspicions that this was more than a straightforward medical case. She had been carried into our twenty-four bed hospital, with her eyes rolling in her head, her mouth foaming, her body racked by convulsions. She hadn't been poisoned. She didn't have cerebral malaria. A medical examination left us none the wiser as to the cause of this life-threatening condition. The sedatives we gave her had no effect. One minute she lay still. The next she thrashed uncontrollably.

Could it be demon possession? None of us were experienced in such matters. All we could do was stand round her bed and engage in spiritual warfare, praying that God would deliver her.

After a while I began paying careful attention to the second hand on my watch. Perhaps it was wishful thinking, but the pauses between her convulsions seemed to be lengthening?

Several hours of prayer later we could see definite signs of improvement. From then on we took it in turns to sit by Akai's bed, praying and reading Scripture. It was a prolonged battle, but after three days and nights she was totally free.

'You have been very sick, but God has healed you. Soon you will be able to go home to your family,' we told her.

And on her face too, there was a look I have never forgotten. The shining look of one in whom the gospel of hope has taken root. 'Me,' she pointed at herself, then caught her pointing hand and clasped it, 'In him.' 'Yes, Akai. That's right. So right.' I could hardly hold back my tears. The gesture she had used was one I had often seen used by those seeking to convey that their lives were hidden with Christ in God.

Henry, the psychologist, had asked me how I felt about life in Turkana. At the time I had been too preoccupied to give him a proper answer. The truth was that those early years were everything I could have hoped for and more. Yes, the lifestyle was arduous. Yes, there were sights and scenes that tore at my heart. But I had such a strong sense of privilege – in being where I was, doing what I did, handling a word of life and power. Where but in Turkana would I see grown men kneeling in the sand weeping and asking Jesus into their lives in response to the gospel message? And my personal sense of awesome privilege was undergirded and enhanced by the fellowship which I had with the other members of the team. Its make-up was somewhat fluid, with a certain amount of coming and going. During my second year in Turkana, Essie got married and a second Mary – Mary Wilson – came to join Mary Moss and me in the bungalow. But the good relationships which had so impressed our visitor continued, nourished not only by our own daily devotional times, but by the pastoral care and Christian example of Dick, our team leader and his wife, Joan.

Every now and again he would call us aside from our busyness for a day of prayer. Of course the work of the hospital continued – patients were treated, emergency operations were performed – but all the non-essential things were set to one side as we sought God's face, seeking his blessing and direction for the future of our work.

Amongst other things such times helped us to keep a grip on our spiritual priorities in the sea of need and heightened our powers of discernment.

A short time after Akai's healing, I was sorting out some paperwork in the house, when Mary came running up the path, the word 'crisis' written all over her normally cheery face.

'Come over to the hospital, Janny,' she begged. 'I'm afraid we may have another Akai on our hands.'

My heart sank. I did not doubt the power of Jesus Christ to deliver, but the intensity of the process placed enormous strain on our physical and spiritual resources. Grabbing my Bible and praying for strength, I followed Mary back to the ward.

Just as my colleague had indicated there was something unusual going on. I heard the peculiar strangled noises, even before I saw the middle-aged Turkana woman who was making them. The beds on either side of her were empty, their occupants having reached their own conclusions. No Turkana would willingly remain under the same roof as an evil spirit.

'Do you think she's possessed? Should we send for Dick?' Mary's questions echoed my own thoughts.

I stood looking at the woman in the bed. She seemed to be trying to say something, but had lost the power of speech. As I watched, it was as if I was suddenly connected up with a memory. I saw myself, sixteen years old, biting through a largactyl tablet, then experiencing its strange paralysing effect on my poor tongue.

'Has this woman, by any chance, been getting largactyl, Mary?'

My colleague consulted the chart. 'Why yes, she has.'

'That's it!' I cried. 'She isn't possessed. She's biting through her tablets.'

The solution was really that simple. From then on the woman was given her medication by injection. Within hours she could speak and her tongue was back to normal.

To me this was almost as great a miracle as Akai's deliverance. I found it particularly reassuring to see that our loving Father did not permit us to embark on a major spiritual battle when a minor medical adjustment was all that was required to solve the problem. Why should I have remembered that particular incident at that particular moment? To my mind this small insight, every bit as much as the dramatic deliverance, bore witness to God's power.

I could go on. Many other experiences spring to mind – all illustrating the adventure, the challenge and the sheer spiritual privilege of those years. Again and again we proved God's power to save, heal and deliver. And in the low times, when the weight of the suffering and the inevitable 'why's', threatened to overwhelm me, there was that safety-net of fellowship and friendship to fall back on.

If there is one image which seems to sum up the special quality of those years, it is of sitting with my missionary colleagues in the open air under the star-studded African night sky singing and worshipping the Lord. The victory of light over darkness was almost tangible at such times – we missionaries, a small group surrounded by velvet blackness, yet warmed by the glow of our fire, our voices raised in simple harmonies, singing out spiritual truth.

Twelve years previously, singing those same choruses around another campfire, I had dreamt of just such a future. Now I sat on this spiritual peak....

Was I happy? Yes – emphatically so. Was I complacent? That is a much harder question to answer. Perhaps for a limited period I did feel I had 'arrived'. Yet before long the Lord was showing me another internal mountain range, crying out to be scaled. It is often an over-simplification when we say 'my thinking changed from such and such a moment'. The point when a fresh awareness starts to make itself consciously felt can be as hard to identify as the moment in a life-history when an individual becomes middle-aged. Looking back, though, I can pinpoint one incident which had a very marked effect.

I had been visiting an outlying settlement for the day, aiming to encourage the few Christians in the area. Recent raids by the Pokot had been the topic of every conversation. People were fearful, wondering when the enemy would strike again. My encouragement to know the peace of God and remember his ability to help in every situation had been well received. And lest this seem super-spiritual, the practical outworking had included cleaning and dressing a huge, horrible, maggot-ridden burn on a man's bottom! Now I was back at the makeshift runway waiting for the little MAF Cessna plane which would take me back to base.

For the first three quarters of an hour I basked in the satisfied feeling that comes with having 'a good day'. But as the sun became a huge red ball, painting the sky with colours only seen in the African desert, my anxiety mounted. The plane should have picked me up long ago. If it did not come within the next ten minutes, it would be too dark for it to land on the rough airstrip, and I would be here for the night.

A gnawing fear took hold of me; the very fear that I had tried to dispel amongst the folk I had been encouraging. What if those ruthless Pokot bandits returned tonight?

Engrossed in my own thoughts, I had not noticed that someone had crept up beside me. Naro was a new Christian, the second wife of a chief who was rather scornful about the new religion which had come into his family. She had been a joy to talk with that day as she seemed so hungry for truth and so radiant in her witness.

'Are you afraid?' came her voice.

'Oh no!' I said quickly.

Her dark eyes searched out mine. And that gentle look uncovered something deep inside me which I had never been aware of before. I was not being honest. I was scared and yet I was pretending I was fine. In those few seconds I realized that through my own words and attitude I was preventing Naro from putting an arm round my shoulders; a comfort for which I longed. If it had been Mary would I have acted that way? If it had been Essie? Or Joan?

I was horrified at myself. It was like the moment of discovery of the first symptoms of some life-threatening disease. A lump. A white insensitive spot. You finger it, trying to persuade yourself it is not what you think.

Yet what else could it mean? This lack of honesty. This unwillingness to show my weakness to national people.

The desert around me grew shadowy. My natural fear cried out for my full attention. But I scarcely heard it, so preoccupied was I with this ghastly revelation. I sat there in my self-imposed emotional isolation, facing and naming a disease I had carried with me from birth.

It was called pride.

5

Tide Of Change

Naro, meanwhile, oblivious to the inner turmoil into which her innocent question had thrown me, was standing a little apart, not wishing to intrude yet evidently unwilling to abandon me altogether.

'I hear the voice of a motorcar,' she observed suddenly.

The chance of a car passing our way was only marginally less remote than that of a white Christmas! Even in the small settlement of Lokori – a veritable metropolis in comparison to this stony wasteland – vehicles were such a rarity that whenever two motorists met on the road they automatically halted to allow their respective drivers to exchange news and handshakes. For my own part I could hear nothing but the chirping and clicking of desert nightlife. I knew, however, that my companion's sense of hearing was a great deal more acute than my own. And if she said she heard the voice of a motorcar then perhaps....just perhaps...I would not be stranded here after all.

Nor was I. Headlamps blazing, engine

roaring, an army Land-Rover eventually filled the horizon and screeched to a halt by my side. It was full of armed soldiers. Angels in heavy disguise?

According to the officer in charge they had been to survey the area after reports of rebel activity and were now on their way to Kapeddo. I did not hesitate. There was a Finnish mission station in Kapeddo. And surely the appearance of a vehicle – any vehicle – bound for a destination from which I could make radio contact with Lokori could be nothing less than providential.

No doubt the officer was somewhat surprised at my request for a lift, but he willingly complied, making a small space between himself and the driver into which I could squeeze.

'Are you not afraid?' he inquired jovially as we set off.

Naro's question again. But this time my answer was totally truthful. 'Not as long as you and your men hold on to your rifles properly,' I laughed.

And my faith was justified. I reached Kapeddo safely, none the worse for my adventure.

Nevertheless the experience had shaken me up. Beforehand if anyone had ever suggested that spiritual and cultural pride could be my stumbling block in the mission field, I would have blinked at them with incomprehension. Was I not relying on the righteousness of Christ and Christ alone for my salvation? Was I not willing to do anything, anything, – the most menial work, the most humble service – to win others to him? How then could I be proud?

My experience with Naro had given me insight. I was proud because my background, my perceived knowledge of the world, yes, even my faith in Christ made me feel – at some level – superior to those with whom I shared it. I had it. They hadn't. Oh dear! I cringed even to spell out this subconscious ugliness in conscious thought.

What was I to do? Back in Lokori I was immediately caught up in the round of administrative duties, of decisions, of ministry. There was little time to pursue the question, let alone come up with answers. But from that time sitting outside my bungalow in evening hours, seeing the gleam of other fires on the other side of the riverbed, I found my spiritual yearnings becoming increasingly horizontal. I longed for a greater mutuality of relationship with the people who had lit them; I wanted to be taught as well as to teach, to be seen as a friend, not just as some cardboard missionary figure with a range of preset Christian responses. The trouble was that with one hundred and one different programmes on the go, the opportunities to relate to the Turkana in such a way were few and far between.

And again my personal soul-searching was one small blip on the broad screen of thinking about world mission becoming current at the time.

This world of the seventies was a very different world from the one in which I had done my missionary training. The map of Africa had changed dramatically, every few years it seemed, seeing the emergence of some new nation with a new name. Many of the leaders of these independent countries were products of missionary training and education, their very sense of nationalism largely the product of Western democratic ideas, based in part upon Christian values. Often they were not hostile to missionaries. Still the relationship between white missionary and newly independent country was very much in the process of definition.

In 1971 a Kenyan religious leader, the Reverend John Gatu, had created a minor sensation in our ranks when he called for the withdrawal of all foreign missionaries for at least five years in order to free the African churches from the bondage of Western dependency and enable them to discover their selfhood. A conference in Bangkok a couple of years later endorsed this call. Whatever the actual response of various missions and missionaries concerned,

75

the fact that such views had been given a public airing left its mark. In the past a missionary going out to teach in a school might have assumed that this was life commitment. Now any such notion of permanency was wiped out.

Our eyes were also being opened to new spheres of service. In the fifties and sixties we talked about evangelized and unevangelized 'countries' – an evangelised country being a country with an indigenous Christian Church. In the seventies we learned to see this as an oversimplification. It wasn't countries that needed to be evangelized, it was 'people-groups' – that is significantly large ethnic or sociological groups of individuals who perceive themselves to have a common affinity for each other. And numerous people-groups might be found in one country, some evangelized, others not.

In Kenya the official response of the Africa Inland Mission to this wave of new thinking had been to turn all its properties over to the National Church and to submit to the authority of its leaders. From 1971 African leaders became largely responsible for assigning missionaries to their various positions of service within the Church and could request the removal of any missionary who, in their eyes, did not seem to be making a helpful contribution. At the same time new missionaries and even those with many years of service under their belts were being actively encouraged to consider pioneering work amongst hitherto unevangelized people groups.

Of course we discussed all these things in the firelight - Dick and Joan, the two Marys and I. To begin with it seemed very far removed. It was all happening out there – in London, in Bangkok, in Nairobi. Our own little world was a world in which we were desperately needed, we had jobs to get on with, people to care for......

But the tide of change crept relentlessly closer.

'Wait till you hear the latest!' Mary came back from a trip to Kalokol, her eyes wide with amazement. Church leaders had requested that two of our missionaries on a nearby mission station should not return there after their furlough.

Most unsettling, that. It was one thing to know power had been handed over. Another thing to see that power being used.

'There's only one way to teach someone to drive. You can give them as many lessons as you like. But there comes a day when you have to give them the keys of the car, let them sit in the driver's seat and take the wheel,' Dick – a firm exponent of the policy of Africanization – said at the time.

And then, suddenly, the swelling tide was lapping round our very doorstep, threatening to carry this godly, much-loved leader from us. The

International Council of the Mission had been looking for the right person to take up the strategic post of Secretary for Outreach into new areas. After much prayer they reached the unanimous decision that Dick should be invited to fill the position. How we prayed!(Striving to set to one side our natural resistance to the prospect of such a loss.) Spiritually we rejoiced when the Andersons decided it was right to accept this challenge. Humanly our hearts were heavy.

'We will miss them so much and yet know deep within our hearts that God is calling them to this new task and we therefore look to him confidently for a new leader in our work in Turkana and for a new doctor for our hospital,' I wrote in my prayer letter.

Little did I realize as I wrote it, that I was still trying to hang onto a past era. There would be no new leader. No new doctor. Not only were Dick and Joan to leave Lokori, but my dear friend Mary Moss as well.

In a few short months our missionary team had been reduced to a shadow of its former self. There was Mary Wilson. And there was me.

Pastor Peter, an African pastor stationed in Lodwar, the administrative centre of Turkana, came to see us. Under the new regulations, as the senior minister in the district, he was our boss. Wizened, weather-beaten and wise, everything about his demeanour suggested that though, like us, he found the situation regrettable, he was not going to waste time bemoaning the depletion in our numbers. Instead, with customary matter-of-fact simplicity, he laid down the ground rules for the future.

'Sister Mary will be in charge of the hospital. Sister Janny will be in charge of the station. And Pastor Amos will be in charge of the church.' Then after a prayer and a cup of tea he left us.

Despite the weight of extra responsibility, this clear delineation of who was in charge of what came as something of a relief. Pastor Amos had recently come to serve in the Africa Inland Church at Lokori and from the outset had conveyed the impression that, as a member of the most influential tribe in Kenya – the Kikuyu – when he was around, power vacuums ceased to exist.

'That was in the time of Anderson. But this is a different time,' he was fond of saying.

And indeed his insistence that we had passed through some sort of watershed was correct. In many ways life continued as before. Hospital administration – medical safaris – clinics. Of course there were cutbacks. Dick's departure left our hospital without a resident surgeon, making us rely even more heavily than ever upon our friends in the Mission Aviation Fellowship to fly in a doctor for one week in the month. Joan had been doing translation work, and it grieved my heart to see that come to a halt.

But these were the surface changes.

The real change, as Amos insisted, was one of order. Up until Dick's departure things had always been done in a certain fashion. It wasn't that he was in any way authoritarian. It was just that he was so experienced, so widely loved and respected, that no-one would ever have dreamt of questioning his decisions.

Now, in the wake of his departure, the voices of small niggles, of secret dissatisfactions found the freedom to make themselves heard. There was a backlash. I don't want to exaggerate – it was neither very loud nor very strong. But it was there...the boat was definitely rocking....and Mary Wilson and I were, metaphorically, holding onto its sides.

A critical wind though discomforting, may also be bracing.

I had trained in a Bible College which laid about as much emphasis on art appreciation as they did upon cross-cultural communication. Only now – over a decade down the road – was I beginning to take a fresh look at some church practices which hitherto I had taken for granted. Might they be reflecting a basic lack of understanding of Turkana culture? At that stage there really wasn't an expert I could question. For another aspect of the problem was that the

African pastors themselves often came from another tribe meaning that they, like me, were exercising leadership in a cross-cultural situation. And like me, they could have benefited from more specific training.

If the thinking of the seventies had been current in the fifties, no doubt that training would have been given. 'West' was not 'best' – we were more sensitive to that now, but we were still reaping the fruits of a less enlightened era with results which could move us to tears of frustration or sometimes laughter, depending on stress levels of the particular day!

Peter's wedding was a perfect example of this.

For several years this rough traditional Turkana man had been in and out of the compound. He was married, but had an extra-marital relationship with a nurse who bore him several children. Still there was a softness about him – a sense of yearning.

Once I felt this so strongly I ventured to speak out. 'Peter,' I challenged, 'When are you going to give your heart to the Lord?'

'Sister Janny, I do not know. But God speaks to me about it almost every day,' he replied.

Not long afterwards he did come very resolutely to faith. And one of the first things he wanted to do (and this without any external prompting) was to regularize his family situation; providing for the nurse and her children, and solemnizing his marriage with his wife, Elizabeth, in church.

Enter the elements of farce. Pastor Amos and his elders had a certain standard for church weddings, which had to be upheld – namely, the bride, whatever her age and former status, should be attired in a full-length white dress complete with veil and matching shoes. 'And who's going to provide it?' Mary asked when she first heard of the ruling, knowing full well that as women, well-versed in such social niceties (from observation if not experience) the buck was passed to us.

We produced the rabbit out of the hat every time. Mary had commandeered the wedding dress of a younger sister and a pair of slingback shoes, and I had always been good with a needle.

Accordingly this dress was taken up, let down, taken in, let out, raised at the shoulders, lowered at the waist, to serve the needs of brides of every shape, size and description. And Elizabeth was no exception. The dress was altered to fit (more or less), the shoes were stuffed with toilet paper, a net curtain served as a veil – and there she was ready to solemnize her marriage in church – except for one thing.

A few days before the happy event the groom was mysteriously absent. Late one night he knocked on our door. He'd been on a shopping expedition to Lodwar – a hundred miles away.

'I bought these for Elizabeth – to wear tomorrow.' He thrust a small brown paper package into my hand.

It contained a black bra, decorated with strawberries and lemons and a bright red pair of pants.

Elizabeth, apparently, was to be one of the few Turkana brides to have underwear! (Pause for further frantic alterations of the dress to try to stop those bra straps showing!)

It was touching. It was funny.

But – as Mary and I were becoming increasingly conscious – it was not the Turkana way.

How ironic that at the very time when I was seeking to shed the racial superiority I had unwittingly carried with me, when I longed to see the gospel take root in Turkana culture free from Western trappings, I should find myself charged with being 'impossible to work with' by an African colleague.

Mary and I had sensed from the moment of his installation that Pastor Amos was the sort of leader, who, conscious of his newfound independence, was anxious to flex his muscles. It soon became clear that in matters of church discipline etc. he would be running a tight ship. This was something we could understand and accept. The trouble was that, coming as he did from a culture where women did not exercise authority, Pastor Amos seemed to feel that he should be running not only the church, but everything else as well. Mary, as a professional in her own field, had the status to back any decisions she made. But it was a lot harder for me. I was in charge of accounts, of a vehicle, of fuel, of supplies of foodstuffs....

Pastor Amos began sending people to me with orders that I should fill their car with petrol or give them a meal – people who really had no claim whatsoever on our resources.

To begin with I followed his instructions. If the unauthorized handouts troubled my sense of good stewardship, they seemed a small price to pay for general harmony.

Then one afternoon a young Turkana girl, a church member, came to visit our house in great distress. I already knew the background to her problem. She had become pregnant outside marriage. A common enough occurrence. But what struck me as less usual was that she had come looking, not for material or financial support, but for spiritual comfort. Her tears were tears of genuine repentance. She knew she had done wrong. She was deeply sorry. Would God ever forgive her?

We spent perhaps three quarters of an hour together talking and praying. And as the girl left I could see she had peace in her heart.

But my own peace was rudely shattered that evening when a very irate Pastor Amos appeared on the scene. Somehow he had heard of the girl's visit. How dare I interfere in church matters! He was the pastor! That girl was a sinner and he, not I, was responsible for disciplining her! On no account was I ever to see or pray with her again!

I can't remember exactly how I responded. No doubt I apologized, explained what had happened, tried to give every assurance that in no way had I intended to undermine his authority. But he left the house unmollified.

Now that the outward semblance of a smooth working relationship had cracked open, deterioration swiftly set in. The pastor and I were clashing. I had to admit it, even to myself. If I had been a man, I believe we could have worked alongside one another. But obviously he felt offended and threatened by the equal footing on which Pastor Peter had placed us. And I, for my part, could not submit to his dominance.

It was a welcome relief when administrative business dictated that I should spend a few days down country. Food was more plentiful there. I would get official supplies, but I also planned to use some of my personal allowance to buy beans – which were so much better and cheaper outside Turkana. I knew that many of my friends on the hospital staff were struggling to make ends meet and I looked forward to being able to resell them at or below cost price.

The trip was made. The beans were bought. Never had I seen such beauties – so firm, plump and purple. All the way back to Lokori I was anticipating the pleasure they would give to my friends.

Pastor Amos was waiting for me on my return, as usual – or so it seemed these days – with a list of complaints. Refreshed by my break, I found it relatively easy to hide the tension his presence always sparked off within me. But the grace wore thin when I saw him eyeing my precious sack of beans.

'I'll take that,' he announced casually.

My heart started beating wildly. Up until now I had never vocally defied him. But this was the limit!

'You most certainly will not. I bought those beans out of my own pocket. They're for my friends.'

'What's here belongs to us all.' He continued to make towards the bag.

'No. Those beans are mine,' I planted my body in his path.

He turned on his heel and I had won the day. But what a sour taste the victory left in my mouth! What a heavy weight on my heart! I hated myself. I hated the beans. I hated the whole complex personality clash in which I had been caught.

And on top of all this there was the sense that,

apart from Mary, there was no-one to whom I could safely unburden myself.

The Mission were bending over backwards to make it clear that they had truly let go of the reins of power. Consequently – or so it seemed to me – only one official interpretation would be placed upon any reports of conflict between white missionaries and African pastors.

The missionary was in the wrong.

Mentally I played and replayed the scenes of conflict. I prayed. I agonized. I lost pounds and pounds of weight.

And finally the crunch came. Pastor Amos went to Lodwar and told Pastor Peter that he could no longer work with me. Whereupon Pastor Peter arranged to visit Lokori, along with a few other church officials, to investigate the problem.

What would they decide? That I was indeed wrong? Reactionary? Impossible to work with?

In those days leading up to the inquiry, I could barely bring myself to look Pastor Amos in the eyes. Their coldness was the most powerful accusation – searing my soul.

6

Ripe For Replanting

The deputation from Lodwar installed themselves under a makeshift shelter outside the pastor's house. Pastor Amos told his side of the story. I told mine. Pastor Peter listened throughout without comment. Then he brought us into the house together and encouraged us to put the past behind us and start afresh. He turned to me: 'Sister Janny, will you forgive this man for any hurts he has caused you?'

The words were like a light shining at the bottom of a long dark tunnel. 'I do – with all my heart,' I gulped.

'Brother Amos,' he turned to the proud young Kikuyu pastor. 'Do you forgive her for the hurts she has caused you?'

'No!' the reply was almost an explosion. And I was in darkness again, weeping silently, as he turned his back.

'Brother Amos!' Gently yet firmly Pastor Peter repeated his question. 'Will you forgive her?'

Pastor Amos studied the ground. 'Not today – maybe tomorrow or the next day,' he muttered.

I came away from the meeting comforted that someone had at least recognized that there were hurts on both sides – but with the pain of a broken relationship still burning within me, and the balm of mutual forgiveness withheld. By the time I went home on furlough six months later Pastor Amos had requested and been given permission to transfer to another church, and I had lost so much weight people thought I was suffering from cancer.

With every bone in my body I had desired a satisfactory resolution to this conflict. There had been none. Now I was in need of all the love and support my sending church could give me. But again my expectations were disappointed. It wasn't that the church folk were uncaring. It was just that no-one seemed to be asking the right questions – the questions that would help me to purge myself of my shame and sense of failure. Instead I was expected to stand up on platforms and talk about the wonderful things God was doing in Turkana. He was doing wonderful things. I could tell of the opening up of the Suguta valley – a vast inhospitable area not far from Lokori as the crow flies, but so inaccessible that no doctor or missionary had ever penetrated its steamy depths before. I could talk of the women's conference in Kapeddo at which I'd watched women from the warring Pokot and Turkana tribes kneel side by side as they sought God with tears, their enmity becoming unity at the foot of the cross.

But to me, during that period, these things almost seemed beside the point. I was hurting inside. Hurting. Hurting. Did nobody see?

And finally I began to get that hurt into perspective. To stand back from it – confront it more rationally – and see what I had learnt.

First I realized that there was a point beyond which I could not hold myself accountable for the way another person handled a conflict; that was his or her responsibility before God. My responsibility was to recognize the faults on my own side – repent of them totally and unconditionally and do my best to put things right. I had done that – therefore I must now accept that God had forgiven me, and forgive myself.

Second I continued to feel that much of my pain might have been short-circuited if I could have found a mature godly Christian who would have leant me a nonjudgmental listening ear. But I stopped secretly bemoaning the fact that no such person was forthcoming. I resolved in future to make a greater effort to be that kind of listener myself, asking the questions that might allow others to give voice to the sort of hurts and problems I had been forced to suppress.

And finally I recognized just how much missionaries – indeed all those involved in Christian work and outreach of whatever description – need to have their relationships covered by prayer. Once I would have been surprised to hear that more people leave the mission field because of relationship problems than for any other reason. But not now. Now I knew from bitter experience just how easily such breakdowns could occur. What's more I realized that this was indeed the strategy of the devil – and had to be prayed against as such. For when a significant work is taking place – and strides are being made for the Kingdom – how better to halt that progress than by sowing seeds of dissension and misunderstanding amongst the work force?

Towards the end of my furlough, when my inner ache was at last beginning to subside, I took greater delight in my speaking engagements. 'Yes, the gospel really is good news to the Turkana people,' I would finish. 'We are seeing God working dramatically, changing hearts and lives. But please keep praying, for the devil is active too. Pray especially that God will give me wisdom and grace as I work with my African partners and cope with everyday pressures and problems....'

So I returned, my self-esteem still bruised, my ideal of partnership in the gospel still battered, my hopes of being humanly heard and understood at some level disappointed. Was I forgetting that God himself is the healer of wounds? The psalmist had put it so powerfully, so simply: 'he restores my soul' (Psalm 23:3).

For me, in this instance, total restoration had not come about as I had hoped through 'time out' and Christian fellowship. But perhaps this disappointment had been permitted for a purpose – so that I might experience my inner healing, in the place where I had got the wound....

In the midst of all the upheaval and adjustment following the departure of Dick and Joan Anderson, I had been very conscious of the folders full of Joan's translation work gathering dust in a corner. This awareness had finally matured into action. It had given me great satisfaction to be able to report in a prayer letter some eight months before my furlough that together with a Turkana helper, under the auspices of the Bible Society, I had taken up the baton – and a first draft of Matthew's Gospel had been completed in the Turkana tongue.

I had concluded that letter by requesting prayer that the Lord would send someone to take over my administrative duties, so that I might give myself full-time to translation and literacy work.

At the time potential administrators were not exactly queuing to come to Turkana and the prospects were anything but hopeful.

Yet now, on my return from furlough under two years later, the desire of my heart had been realized. Two new missionary couples had come to Lokori. They had taken over the general management and administration, leaving me free to get on with the very thing I felt most inclined to do....

This said, I was only too aware of my lack of qualifications. I could type. I had a great interest in languages and a working knowledge of Turkana. But I was not a native speaker. No amount of effort or study could change that. I needed someone fluent in the language and with a deep understanding of Turkana culture to work with me. But suitably educated helpers were like water-holes in the desert – few and far between.

In the months during which I had worked on Matthew's Gospel I had had the perfect assistant in the person of Isaya Emanikor.

Isaya was not a typical Turkana. He was settled, and he was educated. At one time his parents had indeed been nomads, herding their cattle and goats in the traditional way. But then disaster struck. The cattle had died. There had been nothing else for it but for the family to migrate to the Government-designated relief area beside the lake in Kalokol. There the boy Isaya had found himself in a famine camp, learning to catch fish. There Pastor Peter had preached the gospel to him, leading him along with others in his family to faith in Christ. And there Isaya's academic ability had been recognized. He had been sent to school and then to teacher training college. At the time when we worked together on Matthew's gospel he was an active member of the AIC church in Lokori and acting headmaster in the local school.

In the midst of my problems with Pastor Amos, those hours spent in translation work had been an oasis of spiritual refreshment and mental stimulation.

Some of the parables – such as that of the lost sheep – might have been written with the Turkana, whose life and livelihood depended upon the good husbandry of their herds, especially in mind. 'When I was young I looked after animals,' Isaya had recalled. 'I was punished if I lost one, more so if it was a goat. Not because goats are most valuable – they're just harder to find than camels and cows! We all would search and search, sometimes for days, just like the shepherd in the story.'

Yet even where there was such a close parallel between the gospel story and Turkana experience, there was a huge pit for the unwary non-Turkana translator to fall into. 'We can't talk about the shepherd counting ninety-nine sheep into the fold. To the Turkana that is a foreign concept. They never count their animals,' Isaya told me.

'What! Then how do they know if one's missing?' I'd exclaimed.

'They know each one individually – by a dark patch over one eye, or a light strip on the nose.'

Of course 'individually' was exactly the way God knew each one of us. So our challenge had been to find the right Turkana words and images to get that sense into the Turkana version of the story.

With Isaya this kind of thing had been a voyage of discovery.

But Isaya had moved back to Kalakol to take up a well-paid management position with the fisheries department, and now with a less well-educated and committed assistant the work was more of a struggle – and much of the time I feared we were missing the mark.

One morning as I sat at my desk amongst the files and boxes of stencils, the radio crackled to life. A call from Kalakol. From Isaya!

'Janny,' he told me. 'I'm becoming more and more convinced that I should give up my job here and come and work with you.'

The man is mad! That was my first reaction – pure and simple. No Turkana gave up a well-paid job to take up an unpaid position. And Isaya had not just himself, but a wife and two children to think of, not to mention the wider family circle, who in this culture also had a claim on his resources. I daren't encourage him, except in the most general way, assuring him that I would pray about the matter.

Which I did. Isaya meanwhile took definite steps to test his call, initiating discussion with a representative of the Bible Society, Kees de Blois, who was supervising the Turkana translation project. By this time anyone could have seen that the young man was totally in earnest.

Kees, like me, was all too aware of the sacrifice involved. But Isaya was adamant. In our Turkana translation of the Gospel of Matthew, when we had come to Jesus's words: 'Whoever wants to save his life will lose it, but whoever will lose his life for my sake will find it' (16:25), we had used the Turkana word 'abukur', meaning to pour out, as water from a jar, to translate this idea of losing one's life for Christ. And now Isaya was sure that he was meant to pour out his life in the task of translation.

Having established that his wife, Joyce, shared this sense of call, the Bible Society agreed to pay him a salary. It was less than the amount he could have earned in secular employment – as his relatives were not slow to point out. But Isaya would not let this stand in his way. He left his job with the fisheries department, moved with his family to Lokichar – and before I knew it, my position within the Turkana Bible translation project had been turned upside down. I was no longer the boss yearning for a new assistant. Suddenly I was the assistant working with a new boss!

Together, over the next three years, Isaya and I worked on the whole of the New Testament.

As the months went by and we proved ourselves able, without rancour, to sort out our inevitable differences of opinion, and I found myself having no difficulty whatsoever in submitting to his authority, my faith in my ability to live out the policy-ideals being preached by our mission leaders was restored. And this more than anything else was what I needed to heal the wounds of the preceding years.

So the work progressed. Isaya translating. And me typing, stencilling and reviewing. Together we organised review committees with Bible Society linguists and representatives from various Christian groups, to check on the accuracy of the concepts.

If we felt a glow of satisfaction when they pronounced themselves satisfied with the chapters under review, it was more rewarding still to see the reactions of Turkana people, listening to a portion of the Word of God in their own language for the first time.

'This is part of God's book,' I remember telling a group in Kapeddo, as I took the first translation of the epistle to the Philippians from my bag. 'Do you want to hear it?'

There was a loud positive response. The letter had been read to people in other parts of Turkana who seemed to understand it fairly well, but the dialect spoken in Kapeddo was somewhat different.

A little tentatively I began to read, one eye on the page, another on the faces round about me. I came to verse two: 'Grace and peace be unto you from God the Father and the Lord Jesus Christ.'

'Ejok (Thank you),' said a man beside me.

That sounded promising. As I continued, one woman began to repeat every sentence, a definite sign of approval and understanding. With this ongoing background chorus, we reached the end of the letter.

'Greet every saint in Christ Jesus,' I read.

'Yes, we will certainly do that,' came the unanimous response.

'The brethren which are with me greet you,' I continued, scarcely able to keep a straight face.

'Do give them our greetings too,' the people shouted.

There was no doubt about it – the carefully translated words were being heard and understood. I looked forward to giving a positive report to Isaya at our next meeting.

In addition to my work with him, I was now spending several afternoons a week taking adult literacy classes. And these, too, were giving me great satisfaction. The people were so receptive, so eager to learn. Peter's wife Elizabeth (she of the decorative underwear) had become my star pupil; the first non-Swahili speaker to master the written Turkana word, and move into the position where she was able to take classes herself.

It all seemed so right. My longing had always been to see the gospel take root in Turkana culture – and what better way to nurture the seed than by putting the Word of God into the hands of the people, both in the form of complete portions of Scripture and in the early readers produced by the Bible Society especially for use in literacy work?

And then, one ordinary, hot, dusty, busy, fruitful day, the letter came. It wasn't a personal letter – just a copy of a report produced by Dick Anderson, in his new role as Secretary for Outreach into new areas. The new area concerned was that of Namibia, then known as South West Africa.

It began with some background details: the terrain, the system of government, the political tensions, the main exports. It went on to talk about the openings and opportunities for missionary input which had emerged from discussions with church and government officials. Namibia, I discovered, was divided into homelands, i.e. each of the indigenous peoples had been allocated a chunk of land where they had a level of administrative autonomy. Thus the Damara people lived in Damaraland, the Ovambo in Ovamboland and the Herero in Hereroland.

There had been other reports before. Why was

it that from amongst the closely-typed paragraphs of this one, several sentences should immediately catch my eye? They related to the possibilities for outreach to the Herero people. Three Herero tribal chiefs, apparently, had given cautious encouragement in this direction, but insisted AIM should get the consent of their paramount chief before discussing further plans.

Thoughtfully I slipped the sheet of paper into my Bible and got on with the work on hand.

Over the years I have noted that God's guidance has often followed a particular pattern in my life. Every now and then an idea has been thrown in my direction: the opportunity to move into some new sphere of service perhaps. Sometimes I have seized upon it eagerly, my imagination fired with the possibilities. But after a few days or weeks that initial enthusiasm dims, gradually fading into a quiet certainty that the proposal, which may well have been a very good one, was not God's will for me.

But in this case the opposite happened.

Over the next few weeks that report continued to push itself to the forefront of my mind, and in the light of it, I found I was reassessing my present situation. I was enjoying my work. I was convinced of its value. But my aim had always been to make my literacy classes totally indigenous. Elizabeth had proved just how capable the Turkana, once taught to read, were of teaching others. Equally, over the past few years, I had watched Isaya grow in confidence and experience. He no longer needed my moral support. And it should not be too hard for him to find another secretary to do the manual work of stencilling and typing. In other words, in terms of what had become my primary ministry here in Turkana, I was dispensable. While in Namibia.... At that point I could not even venture to finish the sentence. I was too unsure. Could there be a role out there for me?

Eventually I decided to commit my feelings to paper and sound out the General Secretary of the Mission, Maurice Wheatley.

His reply provided exactly the sort of spiritual test I needed to confirm the Lord's call. Yes, he agreed, God did seem to be loosening the soil around my feet – but what was this about Namibia? The AIM Council felt the time had come to have a Mission Secretary in Holland. Would I not consider taking that up instead?

You could have knocked me down with a palm leaf when I read that. Represent the Mission! In Holland! The invitation gave a hugely pleasurable boost to my self-esteem. I was flattered to be asked. I could also see a range of advantages in such a move. Living back amongst friends and family. Escaping from the smells and flies and heat. Taking meetings, organizing. (Two things I greatly enjoyed.) And

101

all in my native tongue! My parents, I might add, were now totally reconciled to my missionary call. Indeed at the celebrations for their fortieth wedding anniversary, which I had gone back to Holland to attend, they had requested that instead of giving them presents, the guests should contribute money towards my work! Yes, at the natural human level everything told me to jump at the chance.

But within twenty-four hours that excitement had faded – the impulse had died. And the closing words of Dick's report were resounding as clearly as ever in my mind. 'Present political tensions in Namibia are considerable. Future developments in Government are uncertain. Military restrictions abound. But it could be that God wants us to build something there for him.' There was no escaping it. I knew I was reading my own name into the 'us' of that final sentence.

I wrote back to Maurice, explaining why I did not feel the job in Holland was meant for me.

Next thing I knew I was opening a letter informing me that an elderly supporter had left me a legacy of one thousand pounds. It was like a spiritual pat on the back – God's whispered assurance that I had done the right thing. My next furlough – in other words 'decision time' – was drawing rapidly closer. Out of the blue I had one thousand pounds in the bank. And I knew exactly how I should spend it.

I went to Namibia for three weeks. Much of that time was spent in Windhoek, the capital, seeing for myself that 'clean, spacious little city, with tall air-conditioned office buildings and beautiful gardens at the centre,' which Dick had described. I stayed with a Swiss couple, John and Yvonne Lubbe, and met many of the committed young black professionals who were part of the lively young church fellowship which gathered for worship in their home.

'Of course it's a totally different story out there in the bush,' the Lubbes told me. 'The parents of these Herero young people are very resistant to the gospel. They were evangelized briefly at the turn of the century by the Lutherans. And now it's almost as if they've had just enough Christianity to vaccinate them against the real thing. We've been praying for so long that God would send people with the patience and the perseverance to reach them. People who could somehow break down the wall of hostility and suspicion, win trust, build relationships and share the word of God....'

Of course I couldn't say too much. But I think they must have realized how deeply attracted I was to this idea. Building relationships – those two words scratched the point of some deep-seated inner itch. The majority of Turkana people, I knew, still saw me as a white benefactor: one who decided whether or not their circumstances were desperate enough to merit material support, one who doled out medicine, who taught them to read, one in authority. And this knowledge sat uneasily with my desire not just to share the Good News, but to embody it, exercising no other power than the power of love.

Now, perhaps, I was being given the opportunity to free myself from the trappings of 'perceived' superiority. To start again from scratch. Going somewhere where I would concentrate first and foremost on people not projects. No aid programmes – no medical clinics – no literacy classes....

Yes, the idea attracted me deeply. But it frightened me too.

I was glad the ultimate decision whether to stay or to move would not be up to me. Nothing would be decided until I could discuss the matter fully with the leaders of the Mission, and with the elders of my home church.

'Goodbye, Janny. Maybe we'll see you again,' Yvonne said hopefully as she and John bade me farewell.

'Yes, maybe,' I replied, my tone deliberately non-committal – but with a smile which probably suggested that deep down I suspected that they would.

managed to make a good start on one of the major languages spoken in Namibia. Afrikaans, with its Dutch roots, did not seem to be too great a hurdle for me. But as far as my main aim was concerned – building relationships with the Herero people – I might as well have sat beside the nearest lake and tried to empty it with a thimble for all the progress I was making. Every day I would walk round the village. 'Wapenduka!' I would call brightly at anyone who came within earshot. But no-one ever responded to my greeting. The Herero women went on gracefully with whatever they were doing without as much as a nod of the head.

How very different it all was from Turkana, I couldn't help but remark. No matter where I'd gone there, I'd been the centre of attention. But the Herero people were well used to whites. They got on with their lives. We got on with ours. That was the way the system operated. So why should they pay any attention to a strange white woman emerging from behind the high chicken-wire fence which surrounded the government compound? Even as I sat on my boulder I felt distinctly uncomfortable about my living-quarters. I understood that this was the accommodation which had been allocated to us, and that our leaders had had no choice in the matter, but in my view, my new home's size and location just seemed to emphasize the very barriers I had been trying to escape. The supremacy of white over black.

With a sigh, I rose to my feet, preparing to take my customary stroll along the dirt path skirting the houses. For the first few weeks my steps had been light, my heart full of hope. I had delighted in the sights and sounds of Hereroland. But these days it took much more of an effort to remain cheerful – more of an effort to try out the few words I had mastered in the Herero language. A dark suspicion was beginning to niggle at the back of my mind. I knew the Herero were a proud, self-sufficient people. Was it possible that I was wasting my time? That my hope of being accepted was a pipe dream?

And then, suddenly, it happened. A woman darted out of her house and rushed up to me, chattering away in Herero. Next thing I knew she was grabbing me by my arm, pulling me over to her home. 'Sit down. Sit down,' her gestures seemed to say. I sat. And yes, she was filling a cup from a kettle. I was being offered tea. Tea! Without the slightest warning, I had become a guest! I couldn't even say thank you – for there is no such word in the Herero tongue. I just took the cup and beamed at my hostess, trying to communicate something of my joy and delight. 'Miriam,' she told me, pointing to herself. 'Miriam,' I nodded happily, almost over-whelmed with gratitude. The tea was the sweetest

I had ever tasted. Not just because it had been made of sugar and water in equal parts, but because it had been made for me by Miriam – my first Herero friend.

From that day on the barriers began to come down. I began to understand that it had not been standoffishness that had prevented the people from answering my greetings for so long. It had been perplexity. Who or what could this newcomer be? A government official? A lunatic? A spy?

Now that Miriam had taken me under her wing, their fears and suspicions were somewhat allayed. But their curiosity, if anything, was heightened. First I met Miriam's family, then her neighbours on either side. One day she made me a bowl of porridge. As I ate I couldn't help but notice the expressions of amazement on the faces of the friends round about. Clearly to the Herero people this was a major departure from the norm. A white woman sitting in a Herero home, eating their food....

One particular question cropped up so often I began to understand it, without the accompanying gesticulations. Why had I come?

'I've come because I want to learn your language so that I can be among you and share the truth of God,' I would reply as best I could in my all-but-nonexistent Herero.

Well it was all too obvious that I didn't stand

much chance of getting anywhere in that respect without their help!

And so one of my long-felt desires began to be realized. I was provisionally accepted – not because of anything I had to offer, but simply because I was there. Miriam allowed me to help around the house, to join her and her friends when they went to collect firewood, to listen in on their chats. Often I returned to base totally exhausted, having spent the best part of the day trying to catch the drift of the conversations which buzzed around me. Just as I had hoped it was all totally different from my experience in Turkana. At one level I seemed to be contributing and achieving little – but I had the sense of laying foundations vital to those relationships I hoped to build. Foundations of openness, of respect, of a growing trust.

During this period Yvonne and John Lubbe continued to be a great encouragement. On one of my visits to Windhoek, Yvonne came up with the idea of a camping expedition. A church member whose parents lived deep in Hereroland arranged that we should go there and stay.

'We'll pack up our sleeping-bags and enough food for a couple of weeks and go. It'll be a really good opportunity for us to improve our language,' she enthused.

And so began a series of profoundly satisfying expeditions into the interior. We learnt so much

– about Herero culture certainly, but also about each other. Lying in our tent in the pitch black, bundled up in several layers of clothes (it was winter by this time – and the temperatures dipped dramatically at night) we shared confidences of the deepest nature.

Yvonne talked to me about her childlessness. She and John had been married for ten years by this stage. They had wanted children but it hadn't happened. She had had to accept that God's will for her life was perfect in this matter – and she was rejoicing in the infant church she and her husband had been given the time and freedom to nurture.

I talked about my singleness. Like Yvonne I knew the pain of not having something that other women had. But I too could see the benefits in terms of ministry. It was easier for the Herero people to receive a single woman into their homes. I was non-threatening. And in this rural situation where there was undoubtedly an element of hostility towards anything that smacked of change (and the 'conversion' religion of white missionaries very definitely fell into this category), I was gaining a place at people's firesides, where a man or a married couple would have been kept at bay.

Still even while I rejoiced in the level of acceptance accorded to me, I was acutely aware of having to separate myself from people as I withdrew into the government compound each evening. How much better if I could have my own little house amongst them. The conviction that this was the way to proceed had been growing within me since my arrival. I had put it to the other members of staff and they had agreed to explore the possibility. But there was a daunting array of obstacles. The very success of the church in Windhoek had served to exacerbate the natural suspicion of evangelical Christianity in rural Hereroland. Parents saw their children change radically – come home with new ideas. And they didn't like it. 'The conversion religion people are stealing our children. Have nothing to do with them,' the word went round. Not surprisingly under such circumstances the Herero authorities were anything but keen to allocate us land.

Yvonne encouraged me to believe that this resistance would be overcome. We prayed earnestly about the matter. 'God will give you a house among the people, Janny,' she predicted. 'It will come.'

A few months later I had to go to Windhoek. As always the Lubbes welcomed me warmly into their home. They seemed in particularly good form that day, despite their many pressures and responsibilities. As we sat chatting at the tea table I watched Yvonne snip off a small bunch of grapes to eat with her fish. 'What a combination!'

I exclaimed. They both laughed and the glow of their happiness struck me more forcibly than ever.

'We have something very important to tell you,' John beamed.

'Yvonne! Are you...don't tell me you're....!'

'Yes.' She rose and hugged me.

The miracle had happened. Yvonne was pregnant.

How we marvelled at God's goodness. At the perfection of his timing. 'Our baby is on its way and your house is on its way too, Janny,' my friend reminded me. Yes, I could see it. Faith is substance, I had been taught in Bible College. That evening I felt convinced that as surely as birth followed conception my dream would become material reality too.

But I had something else on my mind that day – something which I decided not to mention under the circumstances.

I had actually come to Windhoek to consult a doctor about a health problem. And what he had told me during my appointment had confirmed my suspicions. Major surgery was required.

'I'm due to go to the U.K. in September. Can the operation wait until then?' I had asked.

'It could.' The surgeon nodded. 'But if you prefer I will do it for you here – free of charge.'

If you prefer. Three small words – but what a choice. In my Turkana days the decision would have been easy. I would have opted for the comfort and security of home every time. But right from the start my approach here had been different. I was aiming for openness – mutual respect – friendship. Up until this moment I had seen this very much in terms of my living quarters. As that doctor spoke, however, I glimpsed a further set of implications. To be open to people meant sharing myself with them in sickness and in health; it meant entrusting my body to one of their state hospitals; it meant being willing for them to see me in my post-operative weakness....

With the proviso that I would have to have my decision approved by the mission leaders, I accepted his offer.

In March, just under a year after my arrival in Hereroland, the local tribal council approved our request for a plot of ground. Knowing that this was just the first of the official hurdles, I didn't get too excited. Still, it had brought my house one step nearer to materialisation.

The weeks passed....one merging into the next as I gave myself to the task of getting to grips with Herero culture. One day I gave my friend Miriam a bowlful of doughnuts. It was the first time I had ever given her anything and I wasn't sure how she would respond. Yet I wanted to do something to demonstrate just how much I appreciated my welcome to her hearth.

I did not expect to be thanked verbally. I knew that was not the Herero way. Still I was a little taken aback the next day when she wordlessly returned one very sugary bowl.

'OK maybe she didn't have time to wash it, but she might have given it a wipe,' I thought a little ruefully, as I plunged it into hot water.

It was through one of the young people from the church in Windhoek that my eyes were opened to the true meaning of the gesture.

Alfons and I happened to be talking about gifts. 'In Herero culture giving a container back clean means the recipient doesn't want the gift to be repeated,' the young man explained. 'Giving a container back dirty means you like what has been done and hope that it will happen again.'

And there I had been biting back my irritation as I washed my doughnut bowl – when I ought to have been delighting in what my friend was saying about our relationship! Miriam had been placing bricks on the foundation of trust, and I had narrowly avoided knocking them down.

The discovery heightened my awareness of the hidden complexities of communication with those of another culture. We all have a personal grid through which messages of a non-verbal nature pass and by means of which we understand their meaning. In general I considered myself fairly adept at picking up and interpreting

114

these unspoken signals by which others tell us how they really feel. Now I recognized that there was a cultural grid as well; and that it might be a long time before I could pick up and interpret with any degree of assurance the non-verbal signals my Herero friends were sending me.

This knowledge hit me at a time when I was feeling particularly vulnerable. My ongoing struggle to understand the Herero people had awakened in me a deep personal longing to be heard and understood. And yet just when I felt most in need of companionship, it seemed that my main companion was about to be taken away.

Marj Verster, the missionary with whom I shared a house, worked as a teacher in the nearby boarding school. We were much the same age, we got on well, and I valued her friendship. But that May she had received a proposal of marriage from a Christian man with whom she felt she could be very happy, and I found myself struggling to come to terms with this new turn of events.

Once before, in Turkana, I had passed through a similar struggle. Essie, Mary Moss and I had shared a home more than happily for almost a year. We were quite different in personality but had blended together amazingly well. Then the Andersons had gone on furlough, and Dick had arranged for a young Canadian missionary, Wayne Herrod, to keep an eye on Essie and me.

(Mary, too, was away, and mission policy at the time dictated that single women should not be left bereft of male protection.)

I realized almost from the moment Wayne first appeared that Essie was attracted to him. She didn't say much, but she used to disappear regularly with a little stool and her Bible to sit by the river. And, with my ability to pick up non-verbal messages in my own culture, it was not hard for me to guess what was going on in her heart.

Her prayers (and Wayne's too, no doubt) were clearly answered. Wayne was moved away from Lokori, and then providentially transferred back to the area. It was as if the romance had received divine permission to blossom. That autumn the radiant couple announced their engagement.

As far as my own heart was concerned, I had prayed from the outset that God would keep it free from envy. And he had. But it was still very hard to see Essie go, knowing that I would never again have the same quality of relationship with her that we had enjoyed as two single women under the one roof.

Now, just over a year after my arrival in Namibia, it seemed that history was repeating itself with Marj. On the one hand I was truly glad for my friend. It was lovely to see her joy, and share in her excitement. At the same time I had to admit to myself that this gladness was coupled with a small pang. In fact, if I'm to be honest, the pang, though small, was sharp. It definitely wasn't jealousy. It was more an aloneness, an insecurity – the sense that others could walk in and whip away my companions, and that my loss would be the plaintive counterpoint to their gain.

The memory of those late-night conversations when I had spoken to Yvonne about my 'gift' of singleness, now tempted me to wonder how I could ever have been so genuinely positive. Then I had been aware of all the advantages of my single state. Now I saw all too plainly the other side of the coin. And yet even though the temptation to self-pity was strong, God gave me the grace to resist it. I could still look back upon that time when I had laid my fiance on the altar, and know without a shadow of doubt, that, regardless of my current feeling, my present singleness was in his perfect will. I could also look back upon the peace he had restored to my heart at the time of Essie's wedding – and know he could do so again. The only difference this time was my sense of pre-operative vulnerability, which made my longing for someone to lean on – someone who would be there for me permanently – that much more acute.

Finally the day came. As I entered Windhoek State Hospital on 6th June and was shown my bed, I suddenly realized that, but for one brief night many years previously, I had never been on the wrong side of the sheets of a hospital bed before. At Lokori, hospital and patients were part of our daily lives. Over the years I had seen hundreds come and go. This time, however, I was the patient and it felt strange to be on the receiving end of the care and attention.

Operations hold a certain fascination. Anticipated with dread. Chewed over with relish. (It's amazing the amount of medical knowledge you can pick up in a bus queue.) I don't intend to indulge in a blow by blow account of mine. Suffice to say the procedure – a hysterectomy – was followed by fairly major complications in the course of which I was extremely ill.

One interesting aspect is the way the memory of the very real fear, pain and discomfort has faded, while three or four scenes remain sharply imprinted on my mind.

I can still see the basket of flowers that sat on my bedside table. Such luxuries had to be flown in, at great expense, from South Africa. Yet there they were, one of the first things I set eyes on when I came round from the anaesthetic. A glorious array of pinks and blues reminding me of the loving thoughts of my home church in Belfast.

Even more clearly I recall the day my Herero friends (in full national dress) made the three and a half hour journey to my bedside, creating a minor sensation in the mainly white hospital as they sailed in with their gifts – money tied in a rag and a little jar of fat 'to help me grow strong' – and eagerly waited for me to display my scars. Well, I'd come to Hereroland in a spirit of openness, hadn't I? 'There's nothing they haven't seen now,' I thought, halfway between laughter and tears, as Miriam helped me pull my nightdress back over the dressings, amidst much sympathetic clucking from the audience. Once pride had prevented me from receiving the comfort of an African sister's arm around my shoulders. Now I was not ashamed to let those tears spill over. I was thankful – so very thankful – for her embrace.

Most precious of all is a memory from the period of intermittent consciousness which followed a second operation. A little earlier in the day I had been aware of a visitor – Yvonne perhaps – arriving and then leaving again quite quickly in some distress. 'I must be very ill' – the fact registered somewhere in my befuddled brain as reality ebbed away again. The next time I surfaced it was to a similar awareness – of someone standing by my bed – someone whose presence not only eased my physical pain, but gently removed that small sharp lonely pang. How could I have doubted for one moment that I had someone to lean on. I actually felt the gentle pressure of his hand on my forehead.

When the General Secretary rang from London next morning, I was able to take the call myself.

'The Lord has touched me, Maurice,' I told him weakly. 'I'm going to be all right.'

And I was. A few weeks with the Lubbes, a month in Holland and early September saw me back in Otjinene.

Back to language learning....back to gathering firewood....

There had been no major developments in my absence. One small thing intrigued me, though. People in the village had begun to call me by a Herero name.

'They call me "Wahindwa". What does it mean?' I asked Miriam casually as we sat round the fire.

'It means "One who has been sent",' my friend explained.

'Sent? How do you mean – sent?' I persisted.

'Well, sent by God, of course. You have been sent by God, haven't you?'

'Yes, oh yes,' I agreed, my face alight with joy.

What unexpectedly lovely gifts I had seen God give that year. To Yvonne – a miracle baby. To Marj – a surprise courtship. And now to me this new name – 'Sent by God'. A sign that people had ceased to view me as a curiosity – and had worked out, to our mutual satisfaction, who I was.

8

Among the People

The New Year brought further developments. Marj got married. Natanya, Yvonne and John's precious baby daughter, cut her first tooth. And our missionary team in Namibia, which up until the end of '84, had been taken care of by Headquarters in Pietermaritzburg, was given the freedom to appoint its own Field Executive Committee and look after its own affairs.

The work – a joint effort between the Africa Inland Mission and the Africa Evangelical Fellowship – now boasted around twenty missionaries engaged in various forms of ministry. Up in the north of the country, Christian refugees fleeing the war in Angola had organized themselves into small congregations and were looking to the Mission for leadership training and support. In cosmopolitan Windhoek, the little evangelical church was going from strength to strength, having moved from the living-room of Yvonne and John's home into new premises in the black township of Katatura. (Yvonne and John were now planning to move there too.)

We had Christian teachers, such as Marj,

teaching in various secondary schools. Jack and Peggy Pienaar were leading our team, and reaching out into the higher stratas of society. And then, of course, there was my work of pre-evangelism in rural Hereroland.

'Two weeks ago, we had our first Namibian Executive Committee meeting,' I wrote in a prayer letter. 'I am one of the three executive members of this committee and, as there was very little choice, I was made secretary! After our meetings I travelled to Okakarara to work on the minutes and get them stencilled. I enjoyed the job very much as it brought a welcome change to the routine. To start something and actually finish it was an experience I had almost forgotten in my work of trying to befriend the Herero people.'

Yes, that had been an encouragement. But would the discerning reader detect the hint of an underlying problem in my words? A heaviness of spirit? The suggestion that my daily routine had perhaps become something of an uphill climb? They would have been right. At one level I was continuing to rejoice in the quality of the human relationships I had been able to develop. But at the same time after almost two years, I couldn't help feeling there ought to be more – some sign of spiritual development. And on that front, if anything, the news was less positive than it had been six months previously.

In rural Hereroland every little settlement had its 'Holy Fire' – sometimes just a few large stones and a couple of smoking logs – where the people would commune with the spirits of their ancestors. These fires were treated with the utmost respect and played a major part in the ceremonial surrounding births, marriages and funerals.

'Is it right that we should continue to go to the Holy Fire?' was invariably the first question one of the new converts in Windhoek would ask. After my experience in Turkana it was particularly interesting for me to see how this young church approached such matters. The leaders neither rejected traditional beliefs out of hand, nor accepted them without question. Rather these traditions were studied to find out what exactly their meaning was within the culture, and then examined in the light of biblical revelation.

Thus when two young members, Poppy and Alfons, decided they wished to marry there was no automatic ruling that they should substitute a white church wedding for the traditional four day celebration on the bride's compound. Instead the church leaders invited a friend of Alfons' to explain (at length!) the significance of the various customs involved. There followed a Bible study, and a careful evaluation of these festivities. And in the end the whole church decided that the

123

young couple could follow all the traditions (and there were many) save one. The Scriptures clearly prohibited spiritism, and therefore the bride could not be introduced to the ancestors of the bridegroom at the Holy Fire. At that point it was decided that Poppy and Alfons would have a Christian blessing.

Having made this decision, the young people were determined to stick by it. But to their elders, back home, they might as well have declared an intention of digging up their grandparents' graves. They were outraged. And around the beginning of my third year in Namibia, this sense of communal outrage seemed to be reaching a new peak of ferocity. I saw confusion in the eyes of my friends – how could their Wahindwa be a representative of the hated 'conversion' religion? – while in the eyes of the unsympathetic I saw hostility so strong that had I not been single, and a woman, I would surely have been forced to leave. The fact that my solitariness and my perceived ineffectiveness allowed me to continue to be Good News in the area was indeed a privilege. But I had never realized it would prove so costly.

There were times when sitting around the campfire on one of the little settlements deep in the reserve, watching the porridge boil for the evening meal, I would experience a profound contentment: the sense that this was indeed the logical outworking of God's Word to me, that I was where I was meant to be, doing what I was meant to do, with the people I was meant to do it with. But more often I found myself battling with a sense of failure and fruitlessness. I spent hours and hours on my knees pleading for that elusive spiritual breakthrough.

What I actually saw might be described not so much as a breakthrough but rather as a series of cracks in the wall.

Kakauru lived in one of the small settlements outside Otjinene. I had come to know her well through my firewood gathering and tea drinking and she had always been full of laughter, giving the impression she hadn't a care in the world.

And then one day her smile was absent.

'You don't seem yourself, Kakauru,' I observed. 'Is anything wrong?'

It turned out that she had been ill for several days. But what was really troubling her was the fear that she had angered the spirit of her deceased father, and that he had come to kill her.

As seemed to be the norm in Hereroland, my words did not appear to meet the point of her need. She left me uncomforted – and when I called round next day, it was to find that she had been taken to a local 'prophet' who, for a price, would cleanse and release her.

Except his ministrations didn't do the trick. Kakauru got sicker. Her relatives became more and more concerned. And when it grew clear that she was becoming dehydrated, we agreed that she should be taken to hospital in Windhoek.

Times of sickness and crisis are the times when people, whatever their culture, are most likely to look towards a higher power. And so it proved with Kakauru's relatives. That Sunday, with the patient safely between the sheets of a hospital bed, four of them accompanied me to 'the conversion people's church' – clearly prepared to cast their prejudices aside and try anything which might aid her recovery.

They went in warily, driven by anxiety.

They came away touched both by the genuine loving concern of the church members, and by the vitality of their faith.

Kakauru did recover, and went home to her little settlement. No, neither she nor her relatives were converted – but they had softened to the extent that, a few months later, I was invited to come regularly on Sundays to conduct a service in their compound. And as is often the way with such openings, at much the same time I received an invitation to conduct a second Sunday service in the neighbouring settlement of Epata. These services were so small, the entire congregation, including children, could often have been counted on my fingers. And so informal, they would be put on hold if a cow broke loose and totally aborted at the hoot of the mobile shop.

But the fact that they were happening at all was an encouragement. Cracks in the wall of hostility and suspicion were definitely beginning to appear.

Kanji was one of the three chiefs in the area – an old man, steeped in tradition, living deep in the reserve about twenty kilometres from Otjinene. I came to him one afternoon to ask permission to teach the women on his compound to knit. (I had noticed that many of the children were shivering in the early morning cold and knew that the women were wonderfully skilful with their hands.)

'Yes, you may teach them to knit,' he agreed. 'But we'll have none of that conversion religion here.' He pointed over to the smouldering mound beside his hut. 'That's our church.'

I promised that I would tell his women nothing that I wouldn't say to him first, and took my leave. A few weeks later I was back – this time with balls of wool, knitting needles, a sleeping bag and a small tent.

I stayed for ten days, eating and sleeping amongst them. Very soon the women were producing an array of colourful sweaters. Kanji, meanwhile, was clearly beginning to enjoy the novelty of a foreign presence.

First thing every morning he would come over to my tent with a flask of tea and settle down beside me for a lengthy chat. Those breakfast conversations covered a huge range of topics from the distance between America and Russia, to my single state.

'Why aren't you married?' he asked one morning.

'I'm not married because God hasn't given me the man to marry,' I replied.

For some reason this seemed to strike a chord with him. He nodded as if satisfied that this was indeed the correct answer. Did I even glimpse a hint of fatherly feeling in his eyes as he poured my tea?

It was only natural that I should call to see him again – and again.

I'm not quite sure at what stage in the course of the next six months he began to refer to himself openly as my father. I only know that I was more than happy to be considered as an adoptive daughter. Our long talks continued. But our relationship was no longer based on the exchange of words. When he became ill he liked me simply to sit by his bedside, holding his hand.

I felt no sense of triumph on the day he said: 'My daughter, pray with me.' Just a deep joy in the natural, unforced nature of the request. I prayed for him, asking God to give him his truth. I read him story after story from the New Testament. To this day I do not know whether or not he accepted the Lord. But there was definitely some acceptance of something. He clung to my hand, listening intently, until his eyes closed in sleep.

A week after that final visit I heard that he had died.

Funerals in Hereroland are lengthy affairs. It is the custom – and a very healthy one, in many ways – for the mourners to crowd into the house around the open coffin and for the chief mourners to detail incidents from the life of the deceased. Not quite knowing what sort of reception I would get, I donned the traditional Herero dress which Miriam had made me (a huge tea-cosy affair, with several petticoats) and made my way to his home.

There must have been around a hundred women packed into that one square room. I was aware of a turning of heads, a somewhat heightened buzz of conversation as I came in – and then someone took my arm and led me to a space right beside the coffin. The space reserved for family members.

All of a sudden there was silence.

'Wahindwa is going to speak,' said a voice.

I gazed at the face of the old man in the coffin – a man I had grown to love, whose friendship I had greatly valued.

'This is my Herero father,' I told the crowd with a catch in my voice. 'I have talked to him about God and told him of his Son, the Lord Jesus.' I then went on to read from John 14, and

129

to exhort the people to receive God's gift of salvation.

As I spoke there was that unmistakeable quality of silence, which signifies words hitting home. People were attentive – the same people who in other circumstances would have railed against the 'conversion religion'. In the midst of my own sense of human loss, I felt profoundly grateful for this door which had been opened to me. I could only pray that hearts might be open as well.

Another confirmation that ever so slowly progress was being made came when my application for a plot of land in Otjinene received its final official stamp.

'This is one of those days when I write in my diary with large letters and usually in red.' Ecstatically I lifted my pen. 'We first applied for the plot almost a year and a half ago and when I think of all the hassles and the endless obstacles which were put in our way, it is nothing less than a miracle that the land is in our name today. The whole process has been to me like a parable about the work here; strewn with problems, disappointments and outright antagonism. Yet God is victorious and he will triumph if we are faithful.'

There was a flurry of excitement in the neighbourhood that July when my little prefabricated house arrived and was erected by a team of workers. There it stood – a neat three bed-roomed bungalow with an open porch and the drum of a solar heating dish sticking up like a single antenna on the flat roof.

The excitement continued as I moved in, and, with much advice from my colour-conscious Herero friends, decorated, made curtains and bedspreads and gave conducted tours to all and sundry. I got to know my new neighbours. On my right a self-styled prophet would begin beating his drum at around seven o'clock each evening. At the back lived two men who seemed to spend their days tippling the local brew. Between the three of them I could have done with a pair of ear-muffs when I went to bed at night – but I never for one moment regretted the move. Just as I had hoped, living at the heart of that little settlement had opened fresh lines of communication. Now, as well as me going out to visit people, they could drop by and chat with me. Mostly those chats were superficial. What did I think of this piece of material? Would I mind taking photographs of that new baby? Every now and again someone would want to talk about something more serious. But even these rare conversations didn't lead me to believe there was much spiritual searching going on.

Another year passed. The weekly services in Epata and Okotjivango continued. The church in Windhoek made further strides with talk of starting a Bible College. There was a move of the Spirit amongst the mixed-race teachers (officially known as Bastards – a name which in this context had no pejorative connotations) in the local secondary school. One after another a group of six or seven of them came to faith. But amongst rural Herero people – nothing.

I went home on furlough. On my return to Otjinene I started a systematic visitation of the village (approximately 200 houses), leaving in each home a copy of a Scripture Gift Mission booklet 'the Way of Salvation' in the Herero language. I also continued to visit the six little settlements within a forty mile radius, where I had established contacts and built up relationships. But about a hundred kilometres away, near the Botswana border, there was a vast area also known as Hereroland. Jack Pienaar and I had visited it once and met some relatives of a church member in Windhoek, who had seemed open and friendly. 'If I ever come to this part of the world, could I stay on your compound?' I had asked.

That September I felt ready to put their hospitable assurances to the test.

The journey was long, the accommodation (a simple mud hut speedily brushed out) basic, the food about as full of variety as manna in the desert (tea, porridge, the odd potato), but from the moment I arrived I sensed something special about that district. It was as if I had come to plant seeds in ground already prepared to receive them.

Proudly the people led me to a little church on the compound. I looked inside and to my amazement saw furniture: a cross sitting on a table in the centre, old car seats strung around the sides, all covered in dust. It had been built by a man in gratitude to God, my hosts informed me. Nobody really used it – but this Sunday, since I was here, would I be willing to lead worship?

It was a long time since I had taken a service in a church building. It was a long time since I had seen a service in a rural area such as this so well attended. Almost half the population of the small settlement installed themselves on the car seats, and a representative of the absent half of the community had already waylaid me. Some of the villagers didn't feel free to come into the church on account of a family feud, he explained. So when I'd finished would I mind conducting a second service for them in the open air?

One way and another I preached to the entire village that Sunday. And people seemed appreciative, handing me sixty cents in a matchbox to buy bread on the way home, and making me promise to come back – an assurance which I was only too happy to give.

But a veil of anxiety dimmed the smiles of welcome when I next drove into the village. The rains expected ever since my last visit had not come. 'See. It is not good,' the headman drew my attention to the shrivelled bushes and parched balding earth. Indeed it was not good. With so little growth how could the cattle survive? And when the cattle died, what would become of the people?

They knew God as the great Creator, out there somewhere in the unrelenting blue sky, far removed from their everyday concerns. Now I tried to explain that this Creator was a God who longed for intimate relationship with his people. God sees us, knows us and loves us was the message I felt led to bring.

The next morning, from the vantage point of my mud hut at the top of the hill, I noticed a little drama going on. A cow had collapsed outside an old woman's hut. It was obviously very precious to her. She had erected a shelter of corrugated iron to protect its head from the sun, and placed a bowl of water by its side. At her insistence, a group of men were putting ropes round the animal's belly to haul it to its feet and see if it would stand. It wouldn't. The men went away. But the next morning the old woman had them back again – and the next – and the next. Every morning for the next three days the small ceremony was re-enacted. It would have been funny if it hadn't been so pathetic. The men would go through the whole procedure of hauling the cow to its feet and within seconds it would be on the ground again. Cows were dying everywhere. 'Better to kill it,' I could hear them muttering on that third morning.

At which the old woman turned on her heel and came up the path towards my hut.

My heart sank. It was one thing to play the role of sympathetic observer, another to be actively involved.

'Did you not tell us that God is interested in all that happens to us?' the old woman began.

'Yes.' I nodded.

'And did you not read from God's book that Jesus healed all manner of diseases?'

Again I had to agree.

'Will you come and pray for my cow?'

Feverishly I groped for an excuse – but I could find none. I was cornered. The woman was right. The logical outworking of what I had said was that I should pray for her cow. I also believed that I had delivered my message under the guidance of the Spirit and that I had to be open to what God wanted me to do – even if it did make me feel ridiculous.

'All right,' I said. 'I'll come,'

Walking those few hundred yards between my hut and hers was agony. I could see news of the impending 'event' spreading from home to home. By the time I reached the limp animal under its corrugated shelter, the whole community seemed to have gathered round.

I couldn't bring myself to lay hands on it. 'Lord, you see these people. You know this woman's needs. I ask you to heal this cow for your glory,' I prayed – and then hastily excused myself from the scene.

When I next poked my head out of my hut the cow had gone. Dead? Shifted to some other spot? Certainly no-one was rushing to tell me. By afternoon I could control my curiosity no longer. 'What's happened to the cow?' I asked.

'Oh it's over there – walking around,' came the matter-of-fact reply.

I mean, I'd prayed, hadn't I? What else did I expect?

What else indeed? Somehow in my work in Otjinene I'd grown so used to not seeing an immediate answer to prayer that I'd almost forgotten that such answers can and do take place.

God chose to demonstrate his care for that old woman in that particular way. A few days later I was to see him demonstrate his care for the whole village.

I had gone into the little church to pray. A couple of the village women were there with me. As we knelt on that rough concrete floor, the air around us almost crackling with dryness, it was as if their burdens passed onto my own shoulders. I wept, begging God to meet their physical and spiritual needs. 'Lord, please send rain,' I cried.

That night I woke to the sound of a gentle yet persistent pattering on the roof of my hut. The heavens had opened. 'Wakumbe' – 'the woman who prayed' – the people were calling me. I had arrived in a cloud of dust. I drove away through a layer of mud. And on every face there was a smile of thankfulness to God.

Was it a sign? And if so, how should I interpret it?

For some months I had been feeling that there was little more that I could do to progress the work in Otjinene. My house to house visitation was almost completed. When I went to one of the outlying settlements I could almost predict exactly what would happen – who would stop for a chat, what they would say. At the same time I was increasingly aware that whilst I had formed many friendships with women like Miriam, their menfolk were being left behind.

That July Timothy Alford, the former pastor of my home church, and his wife Pansy came to Namibia. And how indescribably glad I was to have Pansy's company while Timothy spoke at a conference – and then to holiday with them. It was such a blessing to have someone at that critical time with whom I could discuss future plans.

The talk on the Executive Council was of John and Yvonne coming to take my place in Otjinene, while I went to live in Arinos, a town not far from Aminius district (where I had prayed for the cow), to begin a new work.

'How do you feel about this, Janny?' Timothy had asked.

'Well...um....unsure.' I strove to sift through my emotions. 'Of course there are still practical details that have to fall into place – like where I should live in Arinos. And it will be hard to leave Otjinene. But I do believe a missionary couple could do so much more here than I am able to do. I suppose really I would ask folks to pray that God will make his way perfectly plain.'

We left it at that. At that point I could not trust myself to convey any more strongly just how desperately I wanted prayer. Travelling around Otjinene with Pansy, I had seen her eyes light up with appreciation at the opportunities to share that were coming my way. Why was it that I could no longer feel a similar enthusiasm? I knew my work had value. But ninety-nine percent of the time that message just didn't seem to be getting through to my emotions. It was as if the slow but genuine upward progress which had been made amongst the Herero people over the past five years had been weighed against an equally slow but unrelenting decline in my sense of personal well-being and spiritual resources.

Four o'clock in the morning – that was the worst time. The house would seem so isolated, the day ahead of me so interminable, the chances

138

of making any progress so remote. And my mind – at least the rational motivating, decision-making part of it – seemed sunk in a miry bog. I couldn't understand it. I had never felt that way before. 'It's the aftermath of surgery,' my doctor had told me when I had tentatively mentioned, several years earlier, that I was feeling low.

I had come back to Otjinene somewhat cheered to know that the mental bog had a physical cause – but wondering what I should do about it.

I was wondering still.

Of course there had been periods of respite. For a few months my spirits would be buoyed up – sometimes through sheer force of will, more often, as now, through outward circumstances. But somehow each respite seemed to leave me a little lower than before.

When the Alfords departed I went back to my empty house. I shut the doors and pulled the curtains and lay down on the bed. For those few weeks their company had provided the respite, allowing me to pretend, even to believe that I was just overtired; that after a relaxing holiday all would be well. But it wasn't. The holiday was over and I was still punctured. Flattened. As empty as a bowl that had been scraped.

I think I knew then that unless I could find some answer to my problem within the next few weeks there would be no new work. No Arinos.

9

Will I Ever Be Normal Again?

My one hope was that my problem might, as the doctor in Windhoek had suggested from the outset, have a physical root. It was now four years since my operation, so the post-operative weakness theory clearly didn't fit the symptoms. But I had also passed through the major hormonal changes associated with the menopause. And this, I knew, could cause general exhaustion and lowness of spirits. I also knew it was treatable.

Thus when a friend offered to take me to Cape Town to consult a doctor there, I grasped the opportunity as if she had thrown me a lifebelt. Something told me, even as I made arrangements for the trip – packing a suitcase, organizing accommodation, booking an appointment – that the course of action on which I had embarked would be decisive one way or another.

That feeling was stronger than ever when, a few days later, I sat in the air-conditioned tranquillity of the doctor's waiting-room. I came out rejoicing. The consultation had been everything I could have hoped for and more. The doctor had been so encouraging. For him my medical history seemed to conjure up a vision of a succession of women arriving in his surgery with symptoms similar to my own and going away in mint condition. 'I'm going to put you on a course of injections.' He had spoken the very words I was longing to hear. 'A few weeks from now, you won't know yourself.'

Nor did I. After the third or fourth injection I thought I was going mad. I couldn't eat. I couldn't sleep. I was hyperventilating and my mind seemed out of control.

Even my confident, urbane doctor seemed somewhat thrown by this unlooked-for development. He promptly took me off all medication and wanted to hospitalize me.

'No!' The reaction was nightmare enough amongst people I knew, without being among strangers.

I went back to the place I was staying to fight my way through. The family I was with couldn't have been kinder or more supportive. They prayed. They sat with me. 'This isn't you, Janny. It's the drugs,' they reminded me time and again.

'This isn't me. This isn't me.' In the midst of the inner tumult I clung to that thought. 'This isn't me.' And if the 'me' somewhere behind all this could just hold on long enough, the drugs would clear my system and I would be free.

Within a few weeks the worst was over and I was well enough to travel home to Holland.

But I still wasn't myself. The drug-induced disorientation had passed, but the underlying problem remained – the depression, the bewilderment. As I sat in the neat bright surroundings of my parents' front room, I couldn't look forward. I could only look back, bleakly contemplating the downward spiral that had culminated in this despair. How had it happened? What had gone wrong?

Obviously there was a physical aspect to the problem. A woman, whose ovaries pack up after major surgery, can hardly expect to sail through the next few years without feeling the draught. And to compound this, in November 1986, while on furlough in Ireland, I had had a second major, though highly successful, operation to remove a prolapsed disc in my spine. With my innate hatred of illness and my resolve never to lie down under anything half a second longer than I absolutely had to, I had really pushed myself to get fit, returning to Namibia in June '87 gloriously free of pain but several months earlier than my surgeon had advised.

In retrospect this was probably unwise. Still, I couldn't help feeling that anywhere other than Hereroland I could have coped. Of course it's harder to get up like a lark when you have a severe pain in your right leg. But I had experienced similar symptoms at home, and in Windhoek, without them bearing in upon my spirit. No, the roots of the problem as I saw it, lay as much in prolonged emotional deprivation and in the psychological pressures associated with my work, as in slipped discs and recalcitrant hormones. The demons which I had battled with year after year had appeared to me far more often in the guise of loneliness and low self-esteem than in physical discomfort and exhaustion.

If only I had had a close colleague working with me, I believed, depression would not have set in. But for much of the time, since Marj's marriage, I hadn't had that support. And although I was indeed part of a missionary team, I felt very isolated – and my work was very different to that of the other team members. They were interested. They cared. But they couldn't really understand the particular pressures I was experiencing. Nor were they there when I came home in the evening, longing to have someone with whom I could share the nitty-gritty of my very ordinary days. If I could have had someone to laugh with....a shoulder to cry on.....

I did have companions staying with me for varying periods of time. But they were new missionaries sent to me for short-term orientation and experience – and tended to add to rather than ease my burdens. Suddenly I would find myself acting as role-model, nanny, and cultural shock absorber all rolled into one.

The Paul/Timothy principle was soundly

biblical and one to which I readily assented. I could see the value and the desirability of passing on some of the things I had learnt in such a way. I could take the girls camping with me in the bush. I could introduce them to my Herero friends. I could explain some of the Herero concepts and thought patterns I had picked up over the years. I could talk about the methods I believed God had led me to use as I sought to witness to the gospel in this gospel-resistant culture.

The trouble was that although I played the part of a role-model, I did not feel like one inside. Naturally the girls would ask questions. Naturally my words and actions were under scrutiny. Technically I was an experienced missionary – but inside I doubted if I had anything to offer. Their observations threatened me. It was as if I half-expected them to dismiss my explanations, to write off my whole ministry as futile.

I felt I had nothing to prove I was doing a good job. No pages of translation work. No list of patients treated and restored to health. Above all no sign that my words were having any marked effect on the lives of the people amongst whom I was living. So what was I doing in Hereroland, a persistent inner voice kept asking? Surely, if my methods were correct, I ought by now to be seeing God's hand of blessing upon my work?

And again I knew this viewpoint was not in line with biblical truth.

The truth was that I was not alone. Jesus was with me.

The truth was that I was in the place of his choosing, doing the job he had given me. My self-esteem should not depend on outward results and human affirmation – but on the knowledge that he loved me and I was in the centre of his will.

I knew this. What was more I knew these biblical truths were the weapons with which I ought to have been able to send the enemy packing. Once before, while at Bible College, I had experienced the power of God's word to release me from emotional bondage. I had been a small child when the Germans invaded Holland during the war. I had watched soldiers stride into our home and thrust their bayonets through the walls. I was deeply aware of the communal burden of fear. 'Sit still. Be quiet. Say nothing.' My own father was hidden in the church. Would the uniformed men discover him? Would they discover the Jews hidden in our neighbours' attic? The fear and trauma of that period had continued to haunt my dreams throughout my teenage years – until the day came when I began to combat those nightmares with the Word of God. I would repeat psalms of praise as I settled down for the night, psalms of trust when I awoke.

And within a few months I was free.

It had worked for me then. Why would it not work for me now? I tried the psalms. I really did. But still the feelings of hopelessness and worthlessness came back...and back. And I was indeed caught in a vicious circle because now in addition to my emotional pain I had to cope with a sense of spiritual failure. Why, when I had done all the things victorious Christians were supposed to do, was I living in defeat?

The burden of all this inner conflict further drained me of energy. During the night I longed for the morning, and in the morning I longed for the afternoon siesta that would permit me to retreat again to my room.

With unkind regularity this hourlong respite would be interrupted by some casual caller. Once this would have delighted me. It had been my greatest desire that people should feel free to come to my home. Now I found myself lying on my bed dreading the knock, unable to rest when it did not come, irrationally annoyed when it did. 'Am I not entitled to a single hour's peace in the day?' the voice of unreason would storm. And instantly I would be guilt-stricken by this reaction, desperately hoping that the girls would not notice that my tolerance level had reached an all-time low. How far removed it all seemed from those days in Bible College when God had given me victory over my irritation with Jenny

147

and over my nightmares of war; when I had been a true spiritual role-model for the incoming students – one who didn't have feet of clay. At that time, and probably for many years afterwards, although I might not have said so in as many words, I suppose I believed that Christians should not suffer from depression. And if they did, it was a sign that they were in some way deficient in their faith.

I had travelled a long way since then.

One of the experiences I found most hurtful during my whole time in Namibia happened when I ventured to share a little of how I was feeling with a trusted friend, and that friend proceeded to suggest that there was something wrong with my relationship with God.

In spite of everything – my lack of motivation, my irritability, my apparent inability to register biblical truth at gut level – I could not accept that. At four o'clock in the morning the one thing that quelled my panic and finally enabled me to get out of bed and face the day was the belief that at some level, beyond the mess of my emotions, God and I were on the same side. That I was serving him. That he was holding me. The suggestion that there was some fundamental flaw in that relationship threatened to sweep away my last line of defence. Mercifully the still small voice of the Spirit was strong enough to reassure me on that score – even before my friend apologized, admitting his diagnosis was most probably mistaken.

Now, sitting in my parents' front room, I still could not feel there was anything amiss in my relationship with God. There was no sin which I could put a finger on. No point over the past five years when I knew I had wilfully chosen to ignore his leading. There was just the over-riding sense that I had been led from a battlefield, bearing the physical and emotional scars of spiritual warfare. A degree of healing had already taken place. But the thought of food still turned my stomach. I still felt as if I was driving with flickering headlights into a future shrouded in fog.

I looked around me, vaguely contemplating the pictures on the walls. Photographs. My sister and her husband on their wedding day. My parents. Me – serene and smiling, the eldest daughter, the well-organized one, the one who had always known exactly what she was going to do.

It was hard to believe that I and that smiling figure in the photograph were one and the same person.

'Oh Lord!' I sighed, lying back in my chair. 'Will I ever be normal again?'

10

On the Scrapheap

'It's lifting. I can feel it lifting.'

The change a few days later, was as sudden and gently dramatic as the moment, on an overcast morning, when the clouds part. One minute I was sitting in a mental fog – and the next I was in sunlight.

General relief all round. 'Some more soup, dear?' I could see the pleasure in my mother's eyes as she saw the relish with which I ate my midday meal. She and Dad had been so anxious – and so forbearing. Doing their best not to appear over-solicitous and resisting the temptation to ply me with questions. I rejoiced for their sakes as much as my own that I was myself again – no longer the pale lethargic inmate of some mental prison.

Now that the doors had opened and I was able to think ahead, I decided to return to Northern Ireland – partly because I knew this would further reassure my parents, but mainly because it was the most natural place for me to be. By 1988 this small troubled patch of the globe had become my adoptive home, and I knew that I would find there the haven I needed to work through the implications of all that had happened over the past few months.

That haven took the very concrete form of a large, gracious house in South Belfast. Its owners, Stanley and Nan Gilmore, were members of Great Victoria Street Baptist Church. Our friendship had begun some ten years previously, when Stanley, over in Nairobi on business, had hired a plane and dropped in to see me in Turkana. (Having committed himself many years earlier to promoting missionary work, Stanley thought nothing of travelling several hundred miles out of his way for the sole purpose of encouraging a missionary. And I was just one in a long line of those on the receiving end of his caring and informed support.)

'You know there will always be a room for you in our place when you're back on furlough,' he'd said at the time.

Down through the years I had frequently and gratefully taken him up on this offer. Staying with the Gilmore family, I discovered, was like stepping up to a closely knit circle, only to discover you are instantly and totally included.

Never had I appreciated this more than in the summer of 1986 when I came home almost crippled with back pain. 'Nothing for it but bedrest. Complete bedrest,' the doctor decreed.

Nan hadn't batted an eyelid. She simply

ushered me to my room, drew back the duvet –
and that was that. For the next six weeks, she
and the rest of the family waited on me hand
and foot. They brought me my meals. They
washed my hair. They read to me. They popped
their heads round the door a hundred times a day
to see if there was anything I wanted. They
encouraged other church members to come and
see me. And when those church members
responded in droves, they ensured that every
visitor to my bedside was refreshed with tea and
home-made cake.

Nor were they in the least put out when all
this tender loving care failed to have the desired
effect on my back (although it did short-term
wonders for my spirits!) and I had to have the
disc surgically removed. My room in the Gilmore
home was still there for me when I came out of
hospital. Stanley and Nan continued to love and
support me throughout my post-operative
convalescence and finally whisked me off for
an all-expenses paid holiday in the sun.

Could anyone ever ask for better friends?

So in the late autumn of 1988, following what
might be compared to the homing instinct of a
pigeon with a damaged wing, I flew back to
them.

And there in the tasteful comfort of their
living-room, sustained by Nan's cooking,
entertained by the children's chat, I worked very

hard at convincing myself that the worst hadn't happened.

One of my deepest fears had always been the fear of failure.

'Will you be going back to Namibia?' well-meaning supporters would inquire cheerfully.

'I'm not sure. Probably not,' I would reply.

'God does not see as man sees,' I would remind myself. Had not Christ's earthly ministry come to an abrupt end when, at thirty-three years of age, he died a criminal's death on the cross? But look at the fruits of that apparent failure!

As long as I could view my years in Namibia in such a light – believing I had been given the strength and grace to keep going for exactly that time-span necessary to accomplish God's sovereign purposes, seeing my return as a stage completed rather than a task aborted, I could banish the evil genie back to the hidden recesses of my heart.

One circumstance was of particular encouragement in this respect. The post of Irish secretary for my Mission Society had just fallen vacant. It was a job I had actually done for a short period before going overseas – involving administration, a certain amount of public speaking, taking a personal interest in the missionary personnel and their needs. It seemed providential that my arrival back in Northern

Ireland had coincided with this vacancy. 'We know that in all things God works for good....' How clearly I seemed to see God working here. If I couldn't go back to Africa, I was sure that serving the Mission in such a capacity would indeed be the next best thing. After talking the matter over with some trusted friends, all of whom were warmly encouraging, I let my name go forward for this home-based position.

A few weeks later I was called for an initial interview with the Irish committee which, I felt, went well. But a second, more searching meeting held early in the new year left me with a vague sense of unease.

There had been a challenging edge to some of their questions. I had answered them as best I could, pointing out the relevance of my experience where appropriate. At the same time I was surprised and somewhat taken aback to realize that I might not, after all, be the 'obvious' choice for the job.

However, once back in the haven of the Gilmore home, I had little time to brood. Stanley, with his businessman's knack of nosing these things out, had discovered there was a good deal on airline tickets in February.

'Nan and I thought we would fly over to Namibia with you, Janny, to help you sort out your affairs,' he mentioned casually one evening. 'I suppose you'll be wanting to stay a few weeks.

We couldn't spare that amount of time away at the moment, but I've spoken to the Ellises, and Maureen is happy to come and keep you company when we leave.'

He made it sound so simple – so matter-of-fact. As if he and the Ellises (also friends from my home church) were talking about a few days at the seaside, rather than a trip to the other side of the world.

And there was nothing I could say except 'thank you'. Up until that moment the knowledge that I must return, if briefly, to Namibia had been an ugly potential trauma lurking in the background. Now thanks to the generous sensitivity of these four friends I could face it with equanimity, knowing beyond a shadow of doubt that if they were in Otjinene with me there would be no replay of the miseries of the past.

We left Ireland on a typical cold grey winter's day.

We stepped out of the plane in blazing sunshine – from which moment life became a social whirl. I wanted my friends to see everything, to meet everyone; Miriam, the members of the church in Windhoek, the Bastard teachers in Otjinene, the rural Herero people living deep in the reserve.

It was so much easier to think in terms of 'introducing friends' rather than 'saying goodbye'. Just as I had expected, Stanley and

155

Nan's presence with me was like a protective covering over my emotions.

Two other factors helped to minimize the trauma of those days. The first was the attitude of the Herero people, who had a nomadic streak in their make-up. They thought nothing of hopping on a vehicle and disappearing off into the bush to stay with relatives for a few months. Husbands could leave home and work elsewhere for over a year – to be greeted upon their return with as little fuss as if they'd just made a trip down to the shops to buy a newspaper. Now you see me! Now you don't! In this culture comings and goings were absorbed into the natural fabric of life. Never for one moment did I get the impression that anyone thought I was deserting them. There were no big farewell scenes as I did my final round of visits. Just the odd gift – a goat here, a couple of chickens there. Everything very happy and relaxed.

And then there was my hard-won little house with all my personal bits and pieces awaiting disposal. How tricky it might have been deciding what to do with them – what to give to whom. But here too my natural feelings were spared. In my absence the house had been ransacked. It still contained some chairs and the kitchen equipment my guests and I required for our stay. It was clean and reasonably tidy – but it was no longer the home I had left. Those thieves had unwittingly aided me in the process of detachment.

Still I was aware of one very sharp pang as I locked the door behind me for the last time. So much prayer – so many hopes – had been invested in that strategically placed little house. It had always seemed central to the progress of the work in Hereroland. But from now on it would be lying vacant. John and Yvonne had spent time in the area. They had prayed long and hard about the possibility of taking over where I had left off but had concluded that this type of rural work was not for them. Essentially they still felt called to a city ministry.

So there would be no-one to follow in my footsteps.

I left Hereroland at one level deeply thankful for the way the Lord had smoothed my path, but at another level deeply disappointed.

'Visitors, Janny! They're waiting for you in the lounge.' Days after my return to Belfast, Nan came running to summon me from my room.

I could tell by the way she spoke that these were no casual callers dropping by to inquire about my trip.

With a pleasurable sense of expectation I smoothed my hair and made my way to the lounge where sure enough two men awaited me. By now my heart was in my mouth. I knew them. They were members of committee who had interviewed me a few weeks previously and from the expressions on their faces they did not appear to be the bearers of good news.

We were part of the same Mission family, and had known each other for many years and the next few minutes must have been every bit as difficult for them as they were for me. There is no easy way to tell someone he or she has not got a job – not even in Christian circles.

The long and short of it was that the Irish committee did not feel that it was God's will for me to become their Secretary.

'A second candidate has accepted the position. We know this will be a disappointment to you, but we believe it is for the best.'

That was the moment when ideally I would have wished to meet them halfway on the bridge of 'God's will', to repay the concern they had shown in coming to see me personally with a brave smile and some expression of faith. But I couldn't. I clammed up. And recognizing that further conversation was likely to be counter-productive, my visitors tactfully left.

The front door shut behind them. Nan returned to her lounge to find me weeping as she had never seen me weep. To say I was devastated would be an understatement. Only once before had something shattered me so totally – the letter in which my fiance expressed his doubts about our relationship. And if anything this was a more bitter pain. For at the time of that earlier disappointment, I still had my missionary call, a relatively untried faith, perfect health and youthful resilience.

Now I was at a much more vulnerable stage.

The decision of the committee seemed to strip me of the last shreds of self-esteem. The recesses of my heart were laid bare. I felt as if I had been fighting a battle with failure – and now failure had won. And I could spiritualize things as much as I liked, but the fact remained: no-one wanted me – I had failed at every level, physically, emotionally, spiritually.

I was redundant – spent – good-for-nothing, on the scrapheap.

I wept and wept and wept.

The scrapheap may be a lonely, soul-destroying place to be. But equally it is a major drag to have a friend sitting on one in the corner of your lounge – even, or perhaps especially, if that friend is someone whom you have supported above and beyond the call of duty for many many years.

By the end of the week Stanley and Nan might have been forgiven for implying, if not directly telling me, to catch myself on – snap out of it – count my blessings. It wasn't the end of the world after all. Just a job. I still had a roof over my head. I still had friends calling to see me. But I couldn't expect them to keep coming if I insisted on being such a misery. So didn't I think, for my own sake as much as anyone else's, I ought to mop my eyes – put a brave face on ....

But they didn't. They didn't say any of these things. Nor did they remind me that 'all things work together for good'. Nan made me cups of coffee by the gallon. Stanley sat for hours, just listening. Family life went on – visitors came and went – and eventually my tears dried up of their own accord.

The failure I had feared and fled from for so long had finally caught me. But it hadn't annihilated me. I was still functional. And I couldn't expect to sit until the Day of Judgement in the corner of the Gilmore lounge.

I got out of my seat that morning, collected my car-keys and powdered my nose. Almost surprised at my own daring, I opened the front door and went out. In the first place I needed some fresh air. In the second I recalled that one of the church members had urged me to drop round.

James MacKeown was the Vice-Principal of Belfast Bible College. I felt mildly ashamed of the way I had treated him during his recent visit. He'd called with a proposal of some sort or other, and had found himself talking to the human equivalent of a seeping brick wall. I knew he knew I hadn't taken in a word. 'At least call in at the college and have a cup of coffee with us,' he had said before leaving.

That much had registered. And now, with a certain limp resolve, I planned to take him up on his offer.

I still felt as if a hole had been blasted in the centre of my being. I certainly didn't expect he could show me how to fill it. But relegation to the scrap-heap didn't absolve one from all social obligations.

Even an abject failure could go and drink a cup of coffee with a friend.

11

Beyond Failure

Belfast Bible College had been founded in 1942. Throughout the fifties and early sixties it had grown in size and influence, weathering a dearth of students in the early years of the troubles, to become widely respected as a centre where Christian workers could be trained to the highest academic and practical levels on a nondenominational basis.

I had passed its former premises – a high narrow house in a built-up residential area – many times over the years, but this was my first visit to its more recently acquired new home on the outskirts of the city. The sights and sounds of community life assailed me as I parked my car in the gravelled park and proceeded to the main entrance. To my right an aproned figure carried scones from the kitchen, to my left students, sporting files of lecture notes and cups of coffee, congregated in small groups in the lounge.

The very familiarity of the scene caused me a pang. Once I had been part of just such a community. Now I was an outsider – a stranger in search of a welcome. Had it been a mistake to take James up on his invitation? Surely the Vice-Principal of such an establishment would have a hundred more pressing things to do than entertain washed-up missionaries to morning coffee. But it was too late for second thoughts. My guide was ushering me to an office where James had already been alerted to my by-now-irreversible arrival.

'Come in. Come in.' His door swung open.

I suppose at some level I must have suspected that this coffee-date might turn out to be something more. But it wasn't until I saw the Principal, Mr. Graham Cheesman, coming in to join us that the full significance of this meeting began to dawn. Gently, almost in words of one syllable (I could see the memory of our last one-sided conversation was as fresh in his mind as in my own), James began to spell out the reason he had been so keen for a chat.

'With over seventy full-time students and around four hundred part-timers, the College is growing and we feel the need for an additional full-time member of staff,' he explained. 'We envisage a new position – that of an 'extension secretary' – being created. We felt that someone with your background and experience would be ideal for the post.'

In other words – I was being offered a job!

With what poise I could muster I finished my

163

coffee, tried to ask the sort of questions that would indicate some grasp of the implications and promised to give the matter my prayerful consideration. Meanwhile, behind the facade of facial and vocal composure, my mind and emotions ran riot.

'Prayerful consideration' conjures up the impression of someone embarking upon a period of controlled purposeful devotional activity, and emerging out the other end with a clear-cut answer. And perhaps for some this is the way it works. My own 'prayerful consideration' took the form of a period during which I told the Lord and anyone else who would listen all the reasons why I couldn't do the job: lack of experience – not knowing enough about the college – ignorance of modern technology – probable inability to relate to students – even more probable inability to relate to other members of staff. (They're academic geniuses, Lord – with strings of degrees!) One objection after another raised its voice to join the underlying clamour of my recently shattered confidence. An extension secretary! Me! Why, I barely felt capable of letting out the seams of a skirt, never mind extending a Bible College. Yet weighted against this negative uproar was the consistent encouragement of close friends and trusted colleagues – and the still small voice of the Spirit urging me to step out....

So I did. Three months after that initial visit to the college, and still with enough reservations to fill a first class restaurant, I found myself at a desk, studying a sheet of paper on which Mr. Cheesman had helpfully outlined the various things he wished his newly appointed extension secretary to do.

'Start a support base for the college,' I read.

'Develop and computerize a mailing list.'

'Prepare a course of lectures on "Introduction to Missions" to be delivered to the Women's Study Fellowship.'

'Lord, what am I doing here! I don't know where to begin!' one part of me wailed.

'Lift your pen. Make a list,' some more robust instinct argued.

So I lifted a pen and headed the first blank sheet of a memo pad: 'Things to do.'

Glancing down the list of items a few minutes later I felt marginally less panic-stricken. Perhaps, after all, I was beginning to see a way forward....but lecturing? Oh I could prepare material all right. I had already compiled a neat outline of topics to be covered and a reading list. But try as I would I couldn't picture myself at the lectern. Would I ever manage to deliver the fruits of my study in ten concise fifty minute blocks?

'Good morning, everyone. As you probably know my name is Janny van der Klis....'

I had reached the watershed of 10.15 a.m. on Monday 6th September – the time and date of my first lecture to the Women's Study Fellowship. There those women sat – and there I stood, exactly as described in the prologue to this book; self-conscious, nervous, torn between the desire to share in a meaningful way, and doubts as to my ability to do so.

The subject I had chosen for that first lecture was the Scriptural mandate for Missions. It took all my powers of concentration to deliver the lengthy opening sentence without stumbling.

'In a rapidly changing world, where new ideas not only in technology but also theology are projected thick and fast, today's missionary needs to have an adequate grasp of the Scriptural mandate for Missions.'

I took a deep breath and began to elaborate on some of the ideas theologians had put forward in recent times. By this stage I was warming to my subject. It was such an important issue. The proponents of this New Theology argued that it was inconceivable that an all-loving God should send anyone to hell, and that humankind's greatest need was to be delivered from the demonic power structures which were destroying their authentic personhood. But, although thought-provoking, nothing I had read in any of

166

these theological works would have convinced me that the understanding of Missions upon which I had based the last twenty years of my life was outmoded. There were biblical concepts at stake here: concepts of the character of God, and the human condition. And now I had forty-five minutes left in which to do them justice – to show how the arguments of the new theology might be refuted.

My lecture did fit neatly into its allocated time space. But one hundred times more important, as I reached the conclusion, I had the satisfaction of knowing that I had not just lectured but communicated. Those women had come with me – I could see it in their faces. They, like me, had been struck afresh by the beauty and the power of Christian doctrine. Together we had traced the missionary mind-set back to its eternal roots.

There was just time for a couple of questions before the partition went back and the coffee cups came in. I wrapped my cold fingers round the steaming brew and sipped gratefully, feeling the warm liquid moisten my dry throat, almost light-headed with relief. In fact I was beginning to suspect that had I not been a missionary, I might have been very happy as a teacher....

Having successfully delivered one fifty-minute block, the next nine seemed much smaller hurdles. Motives for mission, mission and social responsibility, cross-cultural communication, the life of the missionary – these were a selection of the subjects due to be covered. And not only with the members of the Women's Study Fellowship. That March Mr. Cheesman asked me to give a course of lectures to the full-time students. 'The full-time students! Help! I'll never handle their questions!' I panicked. I did handle them, though. And thoroughly enjoyed the additional stimulation.

'It must be wonderful to finish your working days passing on to others what you have learnt over the years,' someone said to me at that time. Wonderful? Well, it was good to realize that those of my students who went on to become missionaries would have a much broader understanding of the task than I ever had. Good to feel that they, with their heightened awareness of all that carrying the gospel from one culture to another involved, could avoid the mistakes of the past and build more effectively to God's glory. But the remark, with its underlying assumptions, still carried a certain sting – the implication that I was on the home straight, the suggestion that I had all my past experiences in some huge mental deep freeze, all neatly labelled, ready to be defrosted and dished up.

How little the speaker really knew me! Outwardly I may have appeared to have slotted into my new role; privately, though, I continued to struggle to come to terms with what had happened. I still carried around within me a great deal of hurt and confusion. Yes, I was enjoying lecturing about Missions: there were models, methods, strategies which I had formerly spelt out to myself in an amateur way. Now I was having to tackle whole books on the subjects. And I revelled in the mental exercise – the challenge of having to stand back from my experience and see how it fitted into the broader theoretical and theological framework. But in some ways my new job only served to highlight all that I had left behind. In the close community of Bible College I knew my place, but the moment I drove through the gates it was another story. Out there in the wider world, suddenly stripped of the official missionary identity with which I had clothed myself for so many years, I felt terribly vulnerable and unsure. It was as if in taking up the challenge of this new position, I had begun to discover that there was a life beyond failure. But I still had to learn how to live it.

And this sort of learning cannot be broken down into convenient fifty-minute chunks for easy mastery. It is long-term – a daily working through of emotions in the light of biblical truth – a series of small positive acts of will – bad days and good days, with the bad days only gradually diminishing in frequency and intensity.

Bishop Handley Moule was once called to

preach at a service for some miners killed in a mining accident in his diocese. During the sermon he showed the congregation the back of a handwoven bookmark with all its raw edges and broken strands of wool. There seemed no sense, no pattern. He turned that bookmark round and the beautifully woven words were plain to all: God is love.

God is love – as long as I could keep my eyes fixed on that side of the bookmark, I found I could live with the broken strands of experience on the other. But it wasn't just a matter of living with them in a spirit of resignation. The temptation when some all-important door inexplicably slams shut is to consider every other door as second best and to allow the energy which could be invested in future service to be swallowed up in regrets. I had to learn to view my broken threads positively – not just giving God permission to weave them into his pattern, but playing my own part in the process. At the most basic level this could mean forcing myself to add names to a mailing list when my natural inclination would have been to brood on the past. Through such acts of will I felt I was demonstrating my desire to cooperate with the Spirit – and this served to strengthen my faith in God's sovereign hold upon my life.

Another important part of my coming to terms with failure was the experiential discovery that

God's love for me was in no way perform-ance-related.

In the months when I felt so unsure whether I had anything to offer as an extension secretary, and when the recent wounds to my self-esteem were still very raw, this message came through loud and clear. So many lovely encouraging things happened: I was provided with a home of my own – the perfect replacement for the little home I had left behind in Namibia. Mine to furnish and decorate, mine to retreat to. And alongside this concrete four-walled testimony to God's care, there were so many smaller ones. Letters. Sunshine. Sermons apparently written with me in mind. Bible readings leaping off the page, all serving to underline the glorious truth – I was loved for being me, not for being successful, effective or even useful. In the past I had experienced God's love as a spur to action. Now it was a cushion for me to lean on while I regained my strength.

This sense of being supremely loved helped me take another important step along the path to restoration. It is tempting, in the face of failure, to look for a scapegoat; someone or something outside ourselves to blame for our pain. From there it is a short step to the pit of unforgiveness – a major progress-stopper.

So in my own journey there came a day of reckoning. I was sitting in my office working on some papers when I heard footsteps on the gravel. I glanced out through the window, and quickly dropped my head. I knew the man – a member of the Irish AIM committee. In all honesty I had to admit that I was tempted to avoid him. But in those few seconds I also sensed that God was presenting me with an opportunity.

'Hello. How are you?' Simple words. A simple greeting. But what a joy to discover that I could smile and hold out my hand towards this brother in Christ, and know that the events of the past few months had not placed any barrier between us. I experienced such a flow of life and power in that moment. If the effort to get up from my desk and take this initiative had cost me something, the spiritual gains were immense.

Of course it is easy to be positive about forgiveness. The place of forgiveness on any spiritual pilgrimage is hardly likely to be queried. But what of those negative emotions – anger, frustration, depression, sorrow – which may continue to dog the traveller, leaping out of the hedge to floor him or her in an unguarded moment, and often (most embarrassingly) in public? Something I had to learn was that these emotions also had their rightful place in the recovery process and ought not to be denied. 'There is a time to mourn,' the writer of Ecclesiastes tells us (Eccles. 3:4). 'Weep with those who weep', St. Paul enjoins in Romans 12:15.

On one occasion it was the showing of a missionary film in our church hall which proved too much for my composure. Africa....those precious relationships....my missionary call. 'I know this is God's will for me. There's nothing wrong. Not really. But it's like a bereavement,' I wept into the arms of a friend. To the untrained eye this might have looked like an emotional setback. Actually it was a means of healing. It was helpful for me to grieve my loss, helpful to be open with my church fellowship about my feelings, helpful to hear others tell me and know in my own heart that this was not sinful, but normal – a normal stage to be passed through in the process of readjustment to life in the West.

So in acceptance of God's will, in leaning on the cushion of his love, in forgiveness of myself and others, in the open expression of grief, I gradually recovered confidence and emotional health.

By September 1990, I could honestly face my strengths and weaknesses as an extension secretary. I was giving the job my best shot. But just as I had suspected from the beginning, it was not completely me. The publicity aspect to my work tended to be more a duty than a joy, whereas in lecturing, in relating to the students and particularly in relating to the members of the Women's Study Fellowship, I was doing something I loved; something which I even dared

173

believe I did reasonably well.

That September I went back to work to discover that due to unforeseen circumstances the co-ordinator of the Women's Study Fellowship had retired.

I remember driving back to my little home in Holywood a few days after this news broke, chatting to the Lord as I changed gear.

'That is one job I would really love,' I told him. 'And I know you can give it to me if it is your will.'

News came down the college grapevine that a couple of people had expressed an interest in the post. It would have been the easiest thing in the world for me to stake my own claim – but I knew that would have been taking matters out of the Lord's hand into my own.

So I contented myself with the jobs on hand: lecture notes, publicity material, an article for a Sunday school magazine. I was sitting at my desk surrounded by papers when Mr. Cheesman knocked at my door. I began to hunt for my publicity file. But he seemed to have something else on his mind.

'I was wondering if you had any thoughts about the post of Women's Study Fellowship Co-ordinator?' he began.

I'm sure I flushed pink, but I struggled to keep my voice calm. 'Yes, I've had thoughts.'

'And....' he pressed me.

'Well...to tell you the truth, I'd just love the job.'

'That's all I need to know. I take it I have your permission to convey those feelings to the Council,' he smiled and left me immersed in a joy as intense as the despair I had experienced in somewhat similar circumstances a mere eighteen months previously.

12

Learning Together

The young woman who sat before me was slim, attractive and clearly uneasy. She fidgeted, glancing past my assistants, Elva and Hazel, towards the door – more like a student expecting to be disciplined by college authorities than an applicant for one of our most popular courses.

With its twin aims of making women aware of their gifts and equipping and encouraging them to use these in God's service, the Women's Study Fellowship attracted a broad cross-section of women from all walks and stages of life. The members followed a three year study course, similar in scope if not in depth to that of the full-time students. They had lectures for three hours every Monday morning and essay-work at regular intervals. On the practical side they were encouraged to play an active part in church life, exploring new areas of service. For that reason one term each year was designated a 'field term', given over to this exploration.

'Sandra, isn't it?' I consulted the form on the table, doing my smiling best to get the interview off to a relaxed start. 'Glad you were able to make it. As we explained in our letter we like to meet every potential student face-to-face for a little chat. So we can get to know them. So they can get to know us. Perhaps you could start by telling us why you feel you want to join the WSF?'

Somewhat hesitantly Sandra met my encouraging gaze. 'Well – I don't suppose I should say this – but I'm not sure whether I do want to,' she began. 'It all started after church one Sunday. I'd gone straight out to the car because I didn't want to have to talk to anyone, when this girl came dashing after me with an application form....'

As the woman recounted her experience, her eyes began to lose their hunted look. She communicated well – with intelligence, insight, even touches of humour. We had already heard stories along similar lines in the course of our interviews that morning. Every intake, apparently, was guaranteed to include its quota of reluctant applicants: those who, hearing about the course, initially resisted the notion of taking the matter further, until suddenly the application form became as hard to ignore as a wailing child, and they finally completed it, ending up in the lecture-room with every appearance of having been ushered in by the Holy Spirit!

But if, in this respect, the background to Sandra's application had a familiar ring there were other aspects which were poignantly individual.

She had watched both parents die of cancer. Her father's death, five years previously, had left her mentally handicapped brother without a full-time carer. Not wishing to see the young man going into an institution, Sandra and her husband felt obliged to take him into their home. They both loved him, but Sandra, who had battled for years with low self-esteem, found the resultant change of lifestyle all but impossible to cope with. She resented the intrusion – and hated herself for resenting it. Stripped of her freedom, the combination of grief, anger and self-hatred finally broke her. She had spent three months in hospital being treated for severe depression.

'I wasn't able to think of doing anything when I came out.' Her eyes shone with tears as she recalled those dark days. 'But recently....I still don't know if I'll be able....but I've begun to feel I'm ready to start building again. And then I heard about the Women's Study Fellowship. And I thought, well, if this is God speaking, maybe I should give it a try.'

'Good for you!'

I had rarely received such a strong impression of emotional fragility combined with immense courage. I could sense a loving heavenly Father longing to take this hurting child in his arms. But would Sandra be able to trust his love sufficiently to take a major step back into the world of human relationships? Clearly this was someone whom Hazel, Elva and I must make the subject of special prayer: that she would return to us in September, that she would rise to the challenge of the course, that the Lord might use the fellowship to meet her particular needs....

By this stage, in June 1992, I had been its co-ordinator for almost a year and a half. And the job was everything I could have hoped for. I was responsible for interviewing and selecting applicants for the September intake of around forty women; for welcoming them along with the second and third year members each Monday morning; for introducing devotions; for co-ordinating the nine lectures which took place; for marking essays and taking care of a multitude of other administrative tasks. Above all I had a pastoral role. And it was in this particular aspect of the work that the promise which I mentioned in the prologue to this book – those words from John's Gospel: 'Gather the pieces left over; let us not waste any' – seemed to be finding its fulfilment. Here the pain of the past had become a well of understanding from which I could draw in my involvement with these women. It provided insight into their needs and a vision of how God could work in their lives. It helped crystallize the means by which the aims of the fellowship might be achieved.

How do we make people aware of the gifts which they have been given to use within the

Church? The general principle that everyone has 'a gift' or 'gifts' is widely accepted. But often we do not become more specific than that. Those with obvious gifts are recognized, while others (at times it would seem the majority!) spend their time defending their choice of a background role. 'I'm not a speaker.' 'I'm not an organizer.' 'I'm no good with kids.' And this may be absolutely true. The problem is that many never move beyond the awareness of who they 'are not' into a positive affirmation of who they are in Christ. Instead of recognizing and developing their own unique spiritual potential, they remain the victims of low self-esteem.

One of my greatest joys as Co-ordinator of the WSF was to help women break free from this negative cycle. If every new intake had its quota of reluctant applicants, the reason for this reluctance was almost always the same. 'I'm not academic.' 'I could never speak in public.' 'I don't know my Bible well enough.' Such confessions regularly slipped out in the course of initial interviews. And every year those who had been convinced of their below-average ability proceeded to amaze themselves: getting to grips with a whole range of subjects which up until then had seemed the province of a theologically educated elite.

There was Betty, a girl so timid, she actually wept as she talked to me. 'I would love to do the course, but I'm sure I can't. Everyone else is so clever, and I'm not.'

'Betty,' I said firmly. 'You can do it. I know you can.'

To obtain their certificate the members of the fellowship had to attend a certain number of lectures each term and do the required essay work. Their essays were marked to the same standard as those of the full-time students, but the results remained confidential, divulged only to the individual concerned.

Often, and usually to the surprise of the essay-writer, the marks were high. Sometimes they were not.

'Look at it this way, Fiona,' I remember saying to one woman who had a real struggle with written English. 'Before you started, what did you know about Christian Ethics? Nothing. You now know 38% more than you used to know. You have gained. That's all that matters.'

Both Betty and Fiona completed the course, and emerged with a new confidence to play an active part in church life. But of course the tendency to compare oneself unfavourably with the rest of the world – or even with one other individual – is not limited to the academic realm.

Ann was one of those people whom it is easy to take for granted – quiet, undemanding, totally reliable. She had seemed to be coping well with the course, enjoying the stimulation. Then out of the blue I received a letter from her. 'Unfortunately I don't think I'm the sort of material for the WSF,' she wrote. 'And after much thought and prayer, I've decided to withdraw.'

What could possibly be behind this? I phoned her and asked her to come and see me.

It turned out that Ann felt a social failure. 'I thought doing the course would make me more.... well....more outgoing,' she confessed.

Suddenly I remembered something. Ann had become very friendly with Cathy – the epitome of chatty extrovertism.

'More like Cathy, you mean....' I prompted gently. Her nod told me all I needed to know.

'Ann, you have been blessed with a lovely personality and so has your friend,' I told her. 'But you're not meant to be her, and she's not meant to be you.'

'No. I suppose not.' Truly this seemed a new thought to this grandmother with over fifty years' experience to her credit. And once Ann realized that a quiet gentle personality could be just as useful to God as an outgoing extrovert one, she no longer wanted to leave. More important she was ready to develop and exercise her own special listening gift.

Encouragement – that was the key. Often all it took was a little encouragement for women to discover that they really did have specific gifts for use in the church, and that those gifts were there to be identified and exercised, with confidence, to the glory of God. For my own part, in knowing from personal experience what it was like to have been starved of encouragement, I could see how God had prepared me to encourage others and I experienced a profound satisfaction in this ministry.

But the encouragement which I gave to individuals on a one-to-one basis was just a small fraction of the encouraging which actually went on in the Fellowship. For fellowship it was. Certainly the study and practical elements were important, and it was wonderful to see the women discovering that there could be more to their Christian service than organizing cake sales and making cups of tea. But perhaps the most significant aspect of our Monday mornings was the half hour of devotions before the first lecture when up to a hundred of us would gather in the long narrow lecture-room. Newcomers to the fellowship were often taken aback by what might have appeared a rather 'selfish' approach to this prayer-time. They would be asked to divide into small groups. 'I don't want you to pray about world issues, or church issues, or even about Mrs. Smith, three doors down, who has just fallen and broken her hip,' I would explain. 'Pray about the things that are touching your own life; is all well in your inner circle? What is God teaching

183

you personally at the moment? Is there an area in which you are struggling? Try to see this half-an-hour as a time when you can share such needs and insights with one another – and together bring them to the foot of the cross.'

I suppose if my experience of the past six years had taught me anything, it had been that the image of the spiritual 'super-Christian' (always smiling, always serene, able to do 'most' things on the strength of one hour's Quiet Time and 'all' things on two) could be as damaging to spiritual health as the image of impossibly slender cover-girls could be to the average woman's self-esteem. God never intended us to cope with every vicissitude of life with the spiritual equivalent of a stiff upper lip. The memory of those dark days in Namibia when I had felt that there was no-one with whom I could safely share my sense of weakness and spiritual failure, now fuelled my desire that these women should be able to be real: with themselves, real with one another, real with God. I wanted them to be able to say where they were hurting.

For many the invitation to share in such a way was initially threatening. I saw expressions ranging from uneasiness to panic on their faces the first time it was suggested. It would have been so much easier to pray for missionaries in Outer Mongolia! Prayer for such worthy causes was part of the Christian apparel they had worn to so many church meetings. And here I was suggesting that they should remove it; give voice to personal needs; perhaps even to admit to areas of weakness and failure.

Of course there was no question of anyone being compelled to bare her soul. But such was the atmosphere of trust, and the example of other members of the fellowship, that the invitation to openness naturally presented itself. And if it was not taken up one week....then it was there again the next....and the next....

'I love Johnny. But he's a difficult child. I get so angry sometimes – and afterwards I feel such a failure.'

'I've been disappointed so often, it doesn't seem worth trying any more. I suppose deep down I suspect God doesn't care.'

'My mother's got Alzheimer's. And of course I would like you to pray for her. But please could you pray for me too....'

Yes it was costly for newcomers to reveal, perhaps for the first time, some hidden anguish. But time and again this kind of honesty proved the doorway through which the Holy Spirit entered their lives. Comforting them. Strengthening them. Helping them to see that God had permitted this need or that problem, neither as an oversight nor a punishment, but in order that they might experience his loving provision 'even there' (Psalm 139:10).

And this restoration of inner wellbeing, in turn, enabled these same members to become more effective in outreach. Far from being 'self-centred', this pattern of prayer and sharing was the means through which the women learnt to minister to one another. It was a vital part of equipping them to use their gifts in God's service.

September came and with it the open morning which heralded the beginning of the WSF year – an occasion when, amongst other things, those about to embark on the course had the opportunity to meet each other and familiarize themselves with the layout of the college.

I was delighted to see Sandra's slender figure amongst the newcomers. It wasn't until later, though, when the fees for the term ahead were being paid, that I was able to make my way to her side. I sensed immediately that a battle was going on. Despite her smile, Sandra seemed anything but happy. It came as no surprise to hear her say she had changed her mind. The course wasn't for her, and she planned to leave without enrolling.

'Yes, I can understand how you feel. It's all pretty overwhelming, isn't it – finding yourself here with so many strangers,' I nodded.

Should I try to dissuade her? I had no wish to manipulate her into doing something against her will. But equally I did not wish her to be held back by the lies the devil commonly tries to tell sufferers from low self-esteem about themselves: that she was worthless, that she would never fit in, that embarking on this sort of course would only add to her problems. I also knew how easy it was for those suffering from depression, or its aftermath, to see God as some sort of slave-driver, seeking to whip exhausted spirits into unremitting effort. I did not think Sandra needed anyone to extol the virtues of fellowship, nor talk of the other women who had felt exactly the same way before enrolling. Instead I simply told her how precious she was to God and how much he loved her, regardless of what she did or did not do. I withdrew then, and left her to make an unpressurized decision.

She did enrol. And afterwards I learnt that our brief conversation had tipped the balance. Every Monday morning from then on, Sandra showed up. She gained confidence. She made friends. She proved to herself how much healing had already taken place in her life. Still, there were times when I could see that she was struggling.

'No-one who hasn't experienced the terrible blackness can really understand,' she told me one morning. 'There are days when I'm fine. And then for no reason I suddenly feel as if everything is closing in – I don't want to see anyone, or go anywhere. It's as if I'm back to square one....'

'Yes, I know,' I found myself saying. 'I know what it's like not to want to get up in the morning. Not to be able to face the day.'

I saw her eyes widen – with surprise, with disbelief.

'Have you had depression?'

'Yes.'

I think for both of us it was a moment of recognition: Sandra seeing herself in me, recognizing that the Lord who had brought her to this point in her journey towards healing, would bring her the rest of the way. Me recognizing, with a small shock of surprise, that I was no longer simply accepting what had happened – I was thankful for it. If anyone had suggested four years previously, as I lay sleepless in the early hours of the morning, dreading the day ahead, that such a time would come, I would have found it hard to believe them. Yet here I was – deeply thankful for the experience which God had entrusted to me, an experience which now enabled me to come alongside this sister in Christ, and ease her sense of isolation.

There is a rich harvest to be gained from times of testing – a harvest of self-knowledge and of experience of God's dealings, a harvest which enables one to reach out to others. I knew that I was reaping it. I also knew from talking and sharing with the other women on the course that many had discovered the same thing.

Standing at the centre of such a fellowship and watching these patterns emerge, I saw again and again that nothing was wasted. I also appreciated more than ever the importance of fellowship – real fellowship – in the body of Christ. What I saw amongst those women seemed to bear out something I had previously suspected: that the main problem which had destroyed my own inner wellbeing and my outward effectiveness in Namibia had been one of isolation. To live victoriously I needed both a real reciprocated relationship with my Creator/Redeemer and real reciprocated relationships with my brothers and sisters in Christ. Yes, to a certain extent I could function without spiritual intimacy with another human being – but, as God himself had remarked in the Garden of Eden: it definitely was not good!

13

I Can't Do It!

I had not resigned from the missionary society when I came to work in the Bible College. The AIM Council had suggested drawing up a secondment agreement, and, at the time, it had been a comfort to feel that I was still considered part of the Mission family. It also meant that everyone knew that at some stage we would be reconsidering my position. Up until the spring of 1992 I had assumed that such reconsideration would probably result in my becoming a permanent member of the Bible College staff. 'Surely I have behaved and quieted myself as a child that is weaned of its mother; my soul is even as a weaned child,' the psalmist wrote in Psalm 131:2, and those words perfectly expressed my state of mind. Weaned of my longing to return to Hereroland, I could happily contemplate the prospect of remaining on the Bible College staff for the rest of my working life.

One thing which had greatly speeded the weaning process was the way the gap in Otjinene had been filled. Denise and David MacIlwaine had both been students at Belfast Bible College. They had two young children and were expecting a third at the time when it was suggested I should speak with them. Bearing this in mind, I had said very little about Hereroland, emphasizing instead the work amongst the Damara people in Windhoek, where the children would be able to go to school. I didn't even permit myself the luxury of a secret 'wouldn't it be wonderful if....' Yet, oh the joy and wonder when they had come back and shared their conviction that Otjinene was the place for them – and I realized that God was indeed calling this couple from Belfast to take my place.

So by that spring of 1992 I had had the tremendous satisfaction of knowing that the little house in the heart of Hereroland was occupied once more, and that the work which I had been forced to leave, was being carried forward. Already there were developments. David wrote of meeting with Herero church leaders. Denise mentioned that two of Miriam's daughters seemed to be professing faith. Such things might not have seemed particularly significant to anyone else. To me they were spectacular – a vindication of all those early mornings when I had told the devil (however weakly and apparently ineffectively) that he was not going to hinder God's work in that place.

Yet there was more.

The letter was lying on the doormat – the first thing I saw when I stepped over the threshold at the end of a busy day. I recognized Maurice Wheatley's precise handwriting on the envelope, and my heart skipped a beat. I knew it could not be an ordinary prayer letter. Why should Maurice be writing a personal letter to me?

The Wheatleys, at that time, were preparing to go to Chad – a predominantly Muslim country in Central Africa, boasting an enormous variety of people groups. One of the projects for which they would be responsible was the setting up of a Centre for African Missionaries i.e. those preparing to take the gospel to neighbouring people-groups. Briefly Maurice outlined the concept behind the Centre. The idea of African witnessing to fellow African was not as straightforward as it might sound. These new missionaries still had to deal with the culture factor. As much as their Western counterparts they faced the challenge of 'contextualization' – even on their own doorstep. So in this Centre Christians who had already received Bible College training were to be prepared for cross-cultural ministry. It was the kind of project which I knew would fulfil a very real need. Still the next bit of the letter all but took my breath away.

Maurice was suggesting that I should consider coming to work at the Centre. There was nothing official about the invitation. He was simply testing the waters. 'If what I have written finds any echo in your heart, you might pursue the matter along the official channels,' he concluded.

My friend, Stanley Gilmore, likes nothing better than to take guests of the family on a drive through the Ulster countryside, introducing them to places of local interest. His itinerary often includes a visit to Scrabo tower – an imposing edifice set on a hill overlooking Strangford Lough. Sometimes the climb to the top scarcely seems worth the effort. The lough is dour grey, the countryside shrouded in mist. And then there are occasions when one reaches the summit only to gasp in wonder at the view – the glorious harmony of land and sky and water.

I think at times God grants us a similar experience in the spirit; moments when we glimpse the breathtaking perfection of ways and thoughts so high above ours. As I folded that letter back into its envelope, I experienced such a moment. I was content. I was fulfilled. I was in no way hankering for change. But Maurice's words had set off not just an echo, but a fanfare in my heart. The moment I read them, it was as if the mist was swept away, and I saw that what I had thought to be my final destination was actually the channel leading to a shimmering, hitherto unsuspected stretch of water – the logical conclusion to the path along which I had been led.

In Turkana God had moulded my attitudes, helping me to appreciate all that is involved in carrying the gospel into another culture. In Namibia I had been given the opportunity to translate that understanding into action – and I had also discovered the cost. In Belfast Bible College I had learnt to articulate the theories which underlay my experience. Now I was being invited to take this body of knowledge and experience and see how God might choose to use it in a new context; assisting a Chadian Principal to prepare African missionaries to reach out to different people-groups within their own land.

The fanfare did not die away. I prayed. I talked the matter over with Trevor Brock, my pastor, and his wife, Barbara – trusted Christian friends, who knew me well. And their advice exactly echoed my spiritual inclination. Every fibre of my being cried: 'Go for it!'

And the doors sprang open. With surprising swiftness my future took on a new shape. The new year of 1993 would not see me teaching in Belfast, but rather studying in Paris – where I was to spend six months learning French, before going to Chad.

En route for Paris I spent a few days in Holland. This gave me a chance to see my family. It also allowed me to attend 'Mission '93', a huge Young People's Missionary conference being held in Utrecht.

It was a welcome opportunity to draw breath, to recharge my spiritual batteries before the challenge of irregular verbs. The last few months had been hectic. In November I had packed up my possessions and let my house. December had been taken up with the normal end-of-term routine punctuated by a string of farewell functions. Swept along on a tide of love and support expressed in gifts, letters, cards (so many from members of the Women's Study Fellowship bearing testimony to the way God had worked in their lives through the things we had shared), I wouldn't have had it any other way. If I was going, I couldn't afford to dilly-dally over turkey and plum-pudding, I had reasoned. I would be fifty-six on my next birthday. The sooner I got out to Chad the better on every count.

Thirty years earlier, in somewhat similar circumstances, I had gone to a meeting hoping for encouragement. On that occasion the Lord had spoken to me through the extraordinary commitment of an ordinary man.

'The servant is not above his master,' Brother Andrew had said. 'He was mocked, ridiculed and eventually killed. Are you willing to give your life to God for missionary service? You may receive the same treatment. Service means sacrifice. There is always a way in. There may not be a way out again. Are you willing?'

Now I was again sitting in a packed

conference-room. And here he was again – like myself, older and greyer. But if I had shut my eyes and simply listened I could have imagined the clock had been turned back. For Brother Andrew was the speaker at that Mission '93 seminar that afternoon, and he spoke exactly the same words as he had spoken over thirty years earlier. Only this time, since the collapse of Communism, his burden was for missionaries to take the gospel to the Muslim world – the world for which I was bound.

Surely this was more than a coincidence! I cannot think of any experience which could have confirmed more strongly both God's intimate knowledge of me as a person, and his sovereign control of my life. I could see so clearly how everything that had happened to date had been part of his plan. There had been plenty of human mistakes on my part – but no divine ones. I was on course – the course which he had mapped out for me.

Was I willing for whatever might lie ahead? Life in Chad would be very different from the life I had enjoyed at home. It was a desperately poor country. I should have to do without many of the luxuries and conveniences I had grown used to in the West. I would face spiritual isolation and oppression. Was I willing? Sitting there, surrounded by so many enthusiastic Christian young people, deeply conscious of

God's faithfulness and power, I knew that all my human securities counted for nothing. Over the past quarter century so many things had changed – but my response to Brother Andrew's question remained the same.

During the next six months I gave myself to study. I enjoy language-learning, but, contrary to what many of my friends seem to think, it doesn't come easily. In my twenties I had pored over an English dictionary. Now, in my fifties, I was poring over a French one – the main difference being that thirty years down the line both body and brain were less elastic. Still I managed to keep pace with my fellow students, and by the end of March I was beginning to feel a little more confident. Everything was going according to schedule. I was hopeful of passing my final exam. My departure date for Chad had been set for 6th September.

On 24th April my father died. His death was not unexpected. He was over eighty, and had been ill for a number of years. I knew it was a mercy that he had died so peacefully. I could even rejoice, because latterly he had discovered the life-giving power of a faith that had once seemed a matter of rules and regulations. The week which I spent at home with my mother, over the time of the funeral, went well. We were sad, tearful at times – but deeply at peace.

I left Holland to return to France convinced that, despite a strange weight on my chest, I was coping well. To be on the safe side, I consulted a doctor, who did a few tests and assured me that the heaviness did not have a physical cause. 'It's a common enough reaction to grief,' he explained. 'Give yourself a little time. It should pass.'

But then, completely out of the blue, I awoke one night, gripped by terror. Only once before had I had a comparable experience, and that had been not long after I moved into my little house in Namibia. Suddenly one evening I had been filled with the most awful fear which seemed to choke me. I cried to the Lord for deliverance and it slowly left, leaving only the memory of horror. It turned out that a powerful witch doctor had started conducting night-time seances virtually at my back door, and I subsequently received a letter from someone who had never written to me before. On a particular evening she had felt a strong urge to pray for me, she explained. She had sensed in her spirit that I was in danger and had pleaded with the Lord to deliver me from evil. The time and the date were just when I had experienced that tremendous fear.

She had been praying for me then. Was anyone praying for me now? This current fear was so strong, I could not stay in bed. Rebuking the enemy in the name of Jesus, I peered out of my bedroom window, hoping to see a light burning in one of the other hostel rooms. But there was none. The minutes ticked slowly by. Three o'clock...half past three.... At four o'clock sounds in the room next door indicated that my neighbour was awake. So desperate was I for spiritual support, that I went in and asked her to pray with me.

By morning my terror had faded, but it was as if the fear was still lurking there in the background, like some evil serpent, waiting to slither out under cover of darkness and wrap me in its coils.

Somehow I got through the final weeks of my course. I sat my exams and passed. But the achievement gave me scant satisfaction. I felt as if I was caught up in an intense psychological battle. One night I had actually heard a voice inside me hurling accusations. I was no good. I never had been any good. Who did I think I was, proposing to go to Chad?

Of course there was a straightforward explanation for my problems. I had experienced a gradual buildup of stress over the past year. I had packed up a house, left a job, launched myself straight into a demanding course, breaking off only to accompany my sister on a trip to Kenya (hair-raising at times) to represent the Mission. On top of this had come my father's death. In other words I had had more than I could take. And my mind and body were protesting. Yet deep down I felt sure this wasn't the whole story. We are spiritual beings as much as physical. And I saw what was happening very much in terms of a spiritual onslaught. I was convinced that the devil had seized upon my natural emotional vulnerability and was exploiting it to the full. In letters I had already told my prayer partners that I was sure he would try to undermine the work in Chad. I had not said this lightly – although, of course, I had not anticipated anything like this.

If I could just get back to Ireland....back into my home fellowship, it would be all right, I told myself firmly. After all there were still two months before I was due to leave. I tried not to think of all that had to be packed into that short space of time. I clung to the word of God, finding one passage in Paul's second letter to the Corinthians that was particularly meaningful. It was the passage in which the apostle describes the enormous pressure he and Timothy came under in Asia – a testing up to and beyond the limits of their endurance.

'But this happened that we might not rely on ourselves but on God who raises the dead,' I read. 'He has delivered us from such a deadly peril, and he will deliver us. On him we have set our hope that he will continue to deliver us....' (2 Cor. 1:9,10).

'He has delivered....on him I have set my hope ....he will continue to deliver....' I tried to make Paul's assertion my own. I was going to Chad, relying not upon myself – but on God. I believed that once the devil saw that nothing he could say or do was going to deter me, he would be forced to withdraw.

For a few days after my return to Northern Ireland it seemed that I had indeed won through. Back in the shelter of the Gilmore's home, I relaxed. I had a week's holiday. My sleep pattern improved. With renewed confidence I devoted the best part of a morning to composing a letter to my praying friends, bringing them up-to-date with my news, and confirming the date of my farewell service.

It was as if that was the signal for the offensive to begin again. I woke up that night so panic-stricken that I had to call Nan from her room. After half-an-hour of intense fear on my part, we sat together in the kitchen. And for the first time I found myself thinking the unthinkable – giving voice to words I had thought I would never say.

'Nan, I can't do it.' I looked at my friend and told her the bald unpalatable truth. 'There's no way I can go to Chad in September – feeling like this.'

14

The Knowledge of His Parenthood

Strangely the moment I said it, I experienced a sense of release – a lightening of spirit. With that one simple admission, a towering, intractable deadline had been swept away. For the first time that year I could look into the future and see an empty pressure-free stretch. Janny the person needed that space, as much as a parched traveller needs water. But what did this mean for Janny the missionary – called by God to go to Chad and specifically trained for that purpose?

Thirty years previously, when I had first heard God's call to share the Good News, the task of reaching people with the gospel had seemed straightforward – a simple matter of commitment combined with conviction and a grasp of biblical truth. In Turkana I had begun to see that there was more to it than that. But it was not until my time in Namibia that I discovered the extent of my limitations and learnt what Paul meant when he said that 'we have this treasure in jars of clay' (2 Cor. 4:7). I had imagined that I would go to Chad with a very different attitude as a result – humbler, more reliant on the power of God. Yet here I was plumbing a new depth of weakness.

As I sat with my friend, facing up to the stark human realities of my situation, I realized, almost to my surprise, that I was no longer panic-stricken. I had a sense of peace and calm, not devastation. 'God has not let this need come into your life to destroy you, but in order that you might prove him and experience his resources.' I had often spoken those words to others over the years. Now I was sensing their relevance to this new set of circumstances. I had reached the end of the resources of willpower that would have got me on that flight to Chad. Spiritually I was willing – but if God wanted me out there, he would literally have to replace my weakness with his strength.

Breaking the news was far from easy. My home church had arranged a farewell service for me on 5th September. Timothy Alford, their former pastor, and now UK director of the Africa Inland Mission, was to have been the guest speaker. Here was a church fellowship ready to give me a sendoff; out in Chad, a team of co-workers were eager to receive me; over in the London office, a number of very busy people had been facilitating the whole process. And here was I, a lone individual, jamming the works. Yet one thing constantly overrode my natural embarrassment. It was the sense that in this very public acknowledgement of my weakness, I was laying the door wide open to God's power. 'For when I am weak, then I am strong' (2 Cor. 12:10). In those days, in a very real way, the truth of Paul's words took hold of my heart.

I also found that I was able to stand back and consider more objectively the dark serpent of fear. I still felt that it was satanic in origin. At the same time I recognized that God must have permitted it to come into my life at that particular time and in that particular way for a purpose; that he had something to teach me through it. What, exactly, at that point, I couldn't quite define. I only knew that when I asked myself in the clear light of a new day how I really felt about Chad, I recognized one very specific area of fear. I was afraid of being alone.

'If I could just be sure of a companion,' I thought. 'I would be all right. I know it.' Of course I had already voiced this need to the Mission staff. They had listened sympathetically and assured me that I had no need to worry. But I did worry. Deep down I had the horrible feeling that their idea of a suitable companion, and my idea, might not be the same thing!

And indeed a few days after all my arrangements had been put on hold, I received a piece of news which confirmed that my anxieties on this score were far from groundless. A fax came through from Chad to the effect that the medical work, which was to have started alongside the

Missionary Training Centre at Ba Illi, had been relocated a hundred miles away. Medical work meant missionary nurses – and missionary nurses meant potential companions; so what that fax told me was that all my potential companions were going to be living one hundred miles down a probably non-existent road.

Somehow this piece of information made everything gloriously and frighteningly simple.

The whole situation had boiled down in my mind to the single issue of companionship. Without the assurance of a companion I knew I could not go to Chad. Yet I still believed that it was God's will for me to serve there. All I could do, therefore, was postpone my departure, wait and trust him to provide.

Towards the end of the summer Stanley and Nan Gilmore made a trip to Kenya where their daughter, Rosemary, was helping an AIC missionary care for handicapped children. The night before they were due to fly back to Northern Ireland, they stayed in Mayfield Guest House in Nairobi – an establishment run, and much frequented, by missionaries.

That morning Stanley didn't feel like breakfast, so Nan went into the dining-room on her own. Shortly after she took her seat, a youthful curly-haired woman filled the single remaining space at the table. In the course of the conversation Nan overheard her mention the word 'Chad', and gathered that this vivacious American had been in that country. On an impulse, without even knowing what missionary society the woman was with, Nan inquired if she had ever heard of Janny van der Klis.

The woman's eyes widened. 'Why sure,' she beamed. 'She's coming to Chad, isn't she? I'm going to be her companion.'

I can't begin to think what the odds against this exchange taking place by chance might be. Certainly, as far as Nan was concerned, chance had nothing to do with it! It was a perfectly-timed answer to prayer. Talking further with Carla (for that was the missionary's name), she discovered that the American had spent the last year and a half working as a nurse in Chad. But latterly she had felt the urge to do less specifically medical work. She was now on her way home on furlough, but would be returning to Chad in June, when it had been agreed she would be based at Ba Illi.

'I'll be spending a few days in England after I leave here,' she told Nan. 'How about you giving me Janny's phone-number, and I'll ring her up for a chat.'

But Nan and Stanley did better than that. They ascertained exactly when and where Carla would be in England; then flew home and informed me that I was going over to meet her!

And so we met, Carla and I. What can I say about that meeting? It was so very precious – so clearly God-engineered. Within minutes we seemed to have known each other all our lives. We even discovered that we were from very similar backgrounds. She had grown up in America – but in a Dutch enclave. She was American/Dutch. I was Ulster/Dutch. As we shared, it became clear that God had taught us many similar lessons in life, and we had the same kind of missionary vision. In short we clicked, with a deeply satisfying spiritual clunk. And I returned to Northern Ireland, recognizing that this bonding would be more than a source of comfort and strength in the days ahead. It was a weapon in the battle against the powers of darkness. And God had ordained that I should wait until that weapon had been forged.

My new departure date was set for January '94. As it turned out the change of plan (which had been lovingly accepted and approved by my home church) had actually come as good news to those already on the field. The work there had not progressed as quickly as expected, and the opening of the Centre for Missionaries had also been postponed.

For a few weeks my profound satisfaction in the prospect of Carla's companionship together with a strong sense of God's leading, dominated

207

everything. I was confident. Positive.

Then, in the post one morning, I received a most unexpected letter from someone I barely knew. Jackie was a newly accepted missionary candidate, who, with her doctor husband, John, was to leave for Africa in the New Year. We had met briefly at an orientation seminar where I had given a talk on spiritual warfare, sharing, by way of illustration, my own recent experience of fear. And now here she was taking me up on it – suggesting that perhaps the whole issue was not as fully resolved as I had sought to convey. 'I know from experience that God can deal with such fear in a radical way,' she told me. 'I am enclosing the telephone number of someone who may be able to help.'

I felt no inclination whatsoever to ring it. Instead I formulated a polite reply in which I thanked Jackie for her concern and explained how God had dealt with my fears. The problem, I claimed, was now behind me. Or was it? No sooner had I sealed the letter than I had an unexpectedly bad night. At first I tried to deny what was happening: this couldn't be the same fear. Not after God had heard my prayers and given me a companion. It must be something else – the fear of fear, perhaps.

But however I classified it, the symptoms became increasingly difficult to ignore. My nights were undeniably restless. The knot of anxiety in my stomach was getting progressively tighter. In the end I was forced to question my assumption that with the provision of a companion all my problems had been solved. God had dramatically provided me with the most compatible of companions, and yet here I was caught once more in the vice of fear.

I was still very loath to ring the number Jackie had sent. I had already spent time with Barbara Brock, my pastor's wife – a trained counsellor – who had talked and prayed with me. What possible benefit could there be in going to bare my soul to a total stranger? All it would take was a little insensitive handling from some so-called expert, and I could end up feeling worse than ever.

'Lord, if you mean me to contact this person – confirm it to me,' I prayed, with very little expectation that he would.

But what I found waiting for me when I returned home to Nan and Stanley's that evening brought me up short. My letter to Jackie had mysteriously reappeared on the hall table.

'Sorry, Janny,' Stanley apologized. 'I took that letter, but forgot to post it. Would you like me to post it now?'

'No thanks. It's a bit out-of-date.' Thoughtfully I fingered the white envelope containing my politely worded rejection of help. Was this God's way of telling me that I needed help from that particular quarter after all?

One thing was sure. The knot in my stomach was still there. It was like an inner parasite at once draining me and driving me. I could concentrate on little else. Finally, in desperation, I made a grab for Jackie's lifeline, fishing the torn bits of her letter out of my wastepaper basket. Still largely against my better judgement, I dialled the telephone number she had sent.

A woman answered. She sounded wonderfully understanding. 'You couldn't have rung at a better time, my dear,' she reassured me. 'Pastor Ray is here and I'm sure he'll be happy to see you.'

The fact that I now felt considerably less-than-happy about going to see him was neither here nor there. I had committed myself to a meeting – for better or for worse.

I suppose what I was most afraid of was that Pastor Ray would be cast in the television evangelist mould; someone oozing confidence and charisma, whose ministrations would leave me cold. That particular fear was allayed the moment the pastor stepped into the room. There was no booming voice, no beaming smile, no slick technique. I found myself looking at a man with an unassuming air and compassionate eyes. 'Would you like to tell me about yourself?' I got the impression that he was prepared to listen for as long as I cared to talk.

'It's one thing dealing with the enemy when he attacks you from without,' he observed when I had explained my problem. 'It's harder to deal with when the attack comes from within. Psychology can often help us analyse and understand things, but only God can heal.'

The most significant thing in my story as he saw it, was that the fear which now haunted me, had surfaced immediately after my father's funeral. It was not the first time someone had pointed out the connection. Barbara Brock had also felt this was in some way significant.

'But I had a good relationship with my father,' I assured him. 'I mean, he knew that I loved him. I was able to tell him so many times before he died. And I know he's gone to heaven. I don't have any regrets or anxieties on that score.....'

'I'm sure you don't. But there could be regrets of another nature.'

We talked for a few hours that afternoon, and then again the next day. Childhood memories came flooding back, bringing with them a hitherto-unacknowledged sense of deprivation. It wasn't just the things I remembered that bothered me; it was the things about which I had no recollection. I could not recall ever sitting on my father's knee. I had no memory of him ever affirming me or telling me that he loved me. He had never openly approved of anything I did. Instead there was one incident which seemed to

211

be imprinted on my memory in Technicolor. I could step back into it, conjuring up the sights, the smells, the feelings, as clearly as if they had happened the day before, rather than fifty years previously.

It was the middle of the war. I was five years old and my youngest brother, Ben, had just been born. Life in our occupied country was hard. Food was scarce. My mother didn't even have sufficient milk to feed the baby. So my father had taken me out on the back of his bicycle into the heart of the country. He had set me down in an area where there were several farmhouses, handed me an empty bottle and sent me off to beg for milk.

'That must have been a frightening experience,' Pastor Ray interjected gently.

'I was terrified. I was afraid of annoying the people in the houses, and I was even more afraid of my father – of his anger if he came back and found I had no milk. But the worst fear was the fear of being abandoned – the fear that he might not come back at all. I felt so alone when he left. Of course it was terrible for him too. He did his best. I know that now....but.....'

Pastor Ray nodded. There were a lot of things I knew at head level. But I was beginning to see that that head knowledge was not sufficient to wipe out the hurt in my heart. The memories were still painful – more painful than I had ever admitted, even to myself.

'What I'm hearing, Janny, is that when you buried your earthly father, you buried the ideal of a father you had never had. And the fear which had entered your life as a five-year-old child was suddenly given a free rein....'

This actually made sense. As Pastor Ray spoke, something slipped into place. I understood.

'I want to take you back to your childhood – in prayer this time,' he continued. 'I feel we should take all those hurts to the Lord and ask him for his healing.'

So we went back to that time and place where I had felt such an acute lack of a loving father. As the pain of it welled up inside me, I sobbed and sobbed. Yet even in the intensity of my anguish, I was aware that I was opening a new area of my heart to God's touch. I was aware of Pastor Ray praying, rebuking the spirit of fear which had taken root in my life; praying against loneliness; praying against everything that had come with that abandonment of a father's love and care.

I felt the knot disappear, as surely as if a surgeon had physically untied something deep inside me. My tears became tears of gratitude. Tears of relief.

'I'll be all right now,' I smiled a somewhat watery smile.

'I know you will,' Pastor Ray smiled back.

Whereupon, in the time-honoured Irish fashion, we sealed it with a cup of tea.

Still the full significance of what had happened did not really hit me until much later that night, when I was alone in my room.

Alone. For so long the very word had had the power to unsettle me. On so many occasions in the past the closing of a bedroom door, the switching off of the light, the sound of my own breathing had been enough to trigger if not feelings of panic, at least a low-level anxiety. But not that night. That night I lay in my bed, utterly at peace. I found myself singing the words of a familiar song, tears of joy streaming down my cheeks. 'Father God I wonder how I managed to exist without the knowledge of your parenthood, and your loving care. But now I am your child, I am adopted in your family, and I will never be alone, for Father God you're there beside me.....'*

Though I'd sung the words many times before, it seemed I'd never grasped their true meaning until now. Only now, after over thirty years of knowing God as my Father, was this wonderful truth sinking in.

I got out of bed and reached for my Bible.

---

*Extract taken from the song 'I wonder' by Ian Smaile. Copyight 1984 Kingsway's Thankyou Music, PO Box 75, Eastbourne, E Sussex BN23 6NW. Used by permission.

There was a verse in Romans which I felt impelled to look up. And here it was – Romans 8:15: 'For you did not receive a spirit that makes you a slave again to fear, but you received the Spirit of sonship. And by him we cry, Abba, Father.'

I repeated those last two words again and again. Abba, Father. Father, Daddy. How had I never seen it before? It was so wonderful. So incredible. This God, the almighty Creator of heaven and earth, was my Dad. The Dad I had always longed for. A Dad who loved me, who approved of me, who placed his arms around me. A Dad who was there for me; no matter where I went; no matter what I did....

I slept that night like a carefree five-year-old, and woke next morning knowing that I was ready for Chad.

15

Scaling the Wall

I had a new assurance, at gut level, that my heavenly Father would not set me a task and then leave me on my own to get on with it. On that basis, a few months later, I boarded the plane for Chad. Relaxing back in my seat after all the farewell flurry, I knew that I was flying to a landlocked, hot and dusty country – one of the poorest on the African continent. Even so nothing in my past experience had prepared me for the sights on arrival.

'It's great to see you, Janny.' Maurice Wheatley met me at the airport. As far as I was concerned he might as well have said: 'Welcome to the wilderness!' I was stunned both by the barrenness of the terminal building and by the rats, scurrying along the road in front of the car headlights, as we drove through what seemed to me mountains of rubbish..

Travelling to the Wheatley's home in N'Djamena, the capital city, my sense of shock grew. The city streets were strewn with litter, the houses all hidden from view behind mud walls. There were no flowers, no parks, no pavements, no traffic system. 'Things will look different in the morning,' I told myself as I went to bed. But they didn't. At 4a.m. a strident wailing torpedoed me into wakefulness. Loudspeakers from the four local mosques were summoning the Islamic faithful to prayer – a summons which seemed deliberately staggered to cause maximum disturbance.

Everything around me appeared ugly and threatening. I'd come to Chad in the holy month of Ramadan – a time during which every Muslim fasts from dawn until dusk. I knew (from my studies) that five times a day the followers of Islam bow down to Mecca, but I still found it disconcerting to see people drop to their knees in the street.

A few days later Maurice left N'Djamena to attend a conference. His wife, Joan, had been in poor health for some time and no sooner had he gone than she took seriously ill during the night. With no emergency services to call on, there was only one thing to do; I had to take a truck and launch out with poor Joan into the chaos of bicycles, mopeds, ox-carts and cars in search of medical help.

Fortunately Joan's condition turned out to be less serious than we had feared, but the experience left me shaken. It had brought home to me the fact that this was a country with neither a health service nor, seemingly, a single comforting, westernized corner to which I could retreat.

217

Could I stick it? That was the question which haunted me during those early days – a question to which all my natural inclinations seemed to reply 'no!' And then, one night, I had a dream.

In my dream I was standing in front of a concrete wall. I wanted to get across it, but it was far too high for me to climb. As I stood there lamenting my plight, I felt someone lift me up from behind. Up and up I went – higher and higher, with me still struggling, until the rugged top of the wall came into view. I reached out to grab one of those rough jutting stones. At that moment I found a foothold, and woke up.

Now I know that dreams are an integral part of sleep, but I rarely remember anything I dream in the morning. This dream, though, was different. Powerful, vivid, immensely comforting, it seemed to represent my loving Father's answer to the fear that I would never cope with life in such a country. The moment I sat up, I reached for my Bible. I opened it at Psalm 18 and looked for a verse I knew was there. 'With my God I can scale a wall' (verse 29).

I took that dream as a divine promise that I could rely on a strength greater than my own to make me equal to the challenges ahead. At the same time recent experience had given me a fresh understanding of the strengthening process. Yes, my Father would strengthen me through his word in the privacy of my own room, but I also had to

218

be willing to turn to other Christians for support.

Carla was not due to return to Chad for another six months. The plan was that we would then set up home together in the bustling village of Ba Illi, close to where the Missionary Centre was located. In the meantime I was scheduled to leave the city and spend two months on an orientation course in the bush. 'Lord, please give me some really supportive Christian friends,' I prayed.

And he did. Within a matter of weeks I had got to know Fran and Sharon, two mature Christian ladies, working with other missions, coming from Canada and USA respectively. Our backgrounds were very different, but our sense of need was the same. We laughed together and prayed together. With them I could freely share my apprehensions and frustrations.

'Janny, we don't have to like Chad, as long as we love the Chadians,' Sharon would say.

Those words were a lifeline as the weeks wore on and the temperatures rose. Chad – the place – might be dirty, dangerous and gruelling, but I was there for its people. Or should I say 'peoples'. For one of the most striking things about the population of Chad was its incredible variety. Researchers had identified around 185 distinctive people groups speaking 120 different languages amongst its six and a half million inhabitants. This indeed was the very reason why the national Church – the Evangelical Church of Chad – wanted a college to train its future missionaries in the principles of cross-cultural mission. They had deliberately located the Centre in Ba Illi because it was a place where many tribes met. Calling into the market there, on a brief introductory visit, I identified dozens of different groupings – each with their own distinctive physiological features and language.

Ba Illi was a cosmopolitan place. Travelling the final 115 kilometres along a dirt road which led to it, though, could be a nightmare. The main problem was that in the rainy season that road became a sea of mud. From July to October you only travelled if you had to, knowing that for every hour you spent inching forward, you would probably spend another totally bogged down.

At the end of June Carla joined me in Chad and two months later we set out for Ba Illi. Anticipating all the difficulties of the rainy season, we loaded up three vehicles with domestic and work-related necessities (items ranging from a plastic bucket to a filing cabinet) and drove off in convoy. The mud was truly indescribable – but we got through, thanks to the backup of Maurice Wheatley and another missionary colleague. The 265 kilometre journey took seven hours and we reached our destination, exhausted and filthy.

Rain poured down throughout the night, and next morning I found Carla in tears. She had spent a wretched night with rain dripping in on top of her from numerous leaks in the roof. Again, because there were two of us, despondency didn't last. Together we got the roof fixed. We waged war on cockroaches and termites. We painted our bathroom. We made our house home.

Meanwhile, three miles away, the first students and their families were arriving at the Centre. Their journeys made our seven hour mud-bath look like little more than a casual jaunt. Most had been on the road for weeks. With no public transport available, they had travelled by ox-cart, on camel-back and on foot. Some had lost the bulk of their possessions en route, but they were uncomplaining. By early September all those who had been accepted for the course had arrived – eight married couples with forty-six children between them.

On the day before term began, I got onto my moped and rode over to the Centre to talk to Moise, the Director, about my timetable. Moise was a Chadian pastor, who had studied the principles of cross-cultural communication in Kenya. I had met him there briefly, and right from that first encounter had sensed that here was a wise, diplomatic and deeply spiritual leader – someone I could respect. A few weeks before he took up his position at the Centre, armed rebels had burst into the weekly market and killed eighteen people. In a nearby village a church was

221

burnt down, as was the pastor's house. None of this had shaken Moise in his confidence that it was right for him and his family to move to the area. He simply remarked that each time he commenced a new ministry, things happened which could have frightened him were his trust not in God. He had an air of strength and serenity that I found deeply reassuring.

But that day when I went to see him I found him with his head in his hands. He looked up at me and I saw not serenity but despair on his face. In the tone of a man who has spent long hours struggling to find an alternative, he told me he would have to shut the Centre before it had even been opened.

'But why?' I stammered.

'Because the students haven't any food and we can't afford to feed them,' Moise explained. 'They used up all their money on the journey. How can they study if they've nothing to eat?'

Back in the village, I reported this to Carla. Of course we were perfectly aware of the principle involved – the principle that the home churches who sent the students were responsible for their support. The principle was a good one but at that moment we knew we had to intervene. Steps could be taken in future to ensure the problem didn't recur. At that moment we threw principle to the wind and emptied our purses, then rushed back to Moise with the money to buy grain.

So the students stayed and lectures got underway. At last I was in the classroom, doing the thing I had come to Chad to do. My great desire was that those sixteen missionaries might find what I had to communicate helpful and relevant. But my French was still far from fluent and it wasn't a first language for the students either. I had to break off at intervals to allow the men to interpret for their wives. The question-time at the end regularly defeated me. More often than not, I hadn't a clue what the questioner was saying. Rather than admit it, though, I hit on a diversionary tactic. 'Would anyone else like to answer that?' I would smile.

Hard – that is the word I would use to sum up those early months. It was hard mentally, trying to convey a body of knowledge and build relationships without the scaffolding of a common tongue. It was hard physically. At night dogs, chickens, goats and neighbours made sure we woke up at least half a dozen times before dawn. During the day I travelled backwards and forwards to the Centre on a little Honda 75. The tyres were not really big enough to get me through the thick sand. Often instead of it carrying me, I ended up carrying it – an activity which was all the more arduous in temperatures of over 90 degrees.

With so much to drain me of energy, I appreciated Carla more than ever. Her vivacious, outgoing personality carried me along. In social situations, when lecturing at the Centre had left my brain numb, I could sit back and listen, while she made conversation. At home our tastes were similar. Once a week we treated ourselves to a really good cup of freshly brewed coffee, served with ceremony and savoured to the full. The little ritual afforded me an inordinate amount of pleasure. I wouldn't have bothered with it, had I been alone.

In October 1994 some speaking engagements took me to Europe for a few weeks. On my return to N'Djamena in early November, a radiant Carla met me at the airport. I knew the moment I set eyes on her that something major had occurred. I also knew that Lanny Arensen, one of our Mission leaders, had come to Chad during my absence. 'We've been friends for a long time – you know that, Janny,' Carla began. 'But now he's asked me to marry him.' Her eyes shone. 'Oh Janny, I'm engaged.'

Engaged! First Essie, then Marj, now Carla. For the third time in my missionary career I was about to lose a companion to marriage. It flashed through my mind that this might be worth advertising. How to meet Mr Right – share a home with Janny van der Klis. But in all honesty that sense of history repeating itself was not my dominant emotion. I was thrilled for Carla and thankful that the news hadn't come as a complete shock. A few months earlier, after hearing on the missionary grapevine that she and Lanny were such good friends, I'd dreamt about their wedding. I'd even shared the dream with Carla and had known from her reaction that she was not adverse to the idea!

No, I had no doubt that this marriage was in the Father's perfect will. Nevertheless the fact that he planned to remove my companion so very soon after giving her to me, was disconcerting. 'Carla will leave here in July 1995 to be married in the USA in October,' I wrote to a friend. 'Which means of course that I will be praying for someone else to share a home and ministry with. Maybe you will pray with me that the Lord will prepare another real companion.'

And yet even as I wrote the words it struck me that somehow that prayer request was not as urgent as it might otherwise have been. Something had changed – quietly but significantly. I'd come back to Carla's news, but I'd also come back to a heartwarming welcome from the college students – from Bousso and Cathérine, from Mattieu and Elisabeth, from Jean and Affia.....

'We've missed you. You belong here.' That was the message I'd picked up from their smiles and hugs.

I remembered how in my dream I'd scaled the wall.

I now sensed those relationships would be my foothold.

16

The View From the Top

In the months after my return to Ba Illi, my French improved. Not only did lectures become less of a struggle, but I was also able to engage with the students in casual conversation. As I got to know them better, it was illuminating to hear how they had come to faith.

Several students, I discovered, had been arrested by the sense of spiritual reality through a dream. One of them, a young man called Abraham, wept as he told us his story. 'I dreamt I had been thrown into a pit,' he explained. 'I knew I was trapped, with no hope of escape. And then a shining figure came and rescued me.' This dream had been the first step in a spiritual journey that ultimately led him to Christ.

So too with Jacob – a man from an unpopular tribe with a predominantly heathen background. He had been a great villain, he maintained, until the night he dreamt of a Christlike figure rescuing him from a burning house. Suddenly aware of his need to be forgiven, he sought the help of a local Christian pastor. In this way, again through the initial prompting of a dream, Jacob became a Christian.

I suppose up until that time I had hardly noticed the number of occasions on which God had spoken to people through dreams in the Scriptures. Now, listening to the students and reflecting upon my own recent experience, I began to see that dreams could be a method he still used to communicate today. Indeed I saw the great value of this method as a means of preparing illiterate people to receive the spiritual truth of his Word.

Another thing that struck me, as I got to know the students, was the depth and strength of their commitment. I'd been aware from the outset that they were mature believers. Each couple had been chosen by their local churches and accepted by the Missionary Society of the Evangelical Church of Chad. Most had come from the South Western corner of the country, where the Christian church is strong both numerically and spiritually.

'That scar on Valery's head – how did he get it? Was he in an accident?' I happened to ask one day.

'No. It wasn't an accident,' came the matter-of-fact reply. 'He was attacked because he was a Christian. They buried him up to his neck in sand and hit him on the head with a spade.'

It transpired that Valery's scar dated back to a period in the late seventies when a heathen President had passed a series of anti-Christian laws. He had imposed restrictions on church services, abolished Christian holidays and festivals and forced believers to retract their Christian names. In such a climate physical attacks were common and many believers lost their lives. Now, twenty years on, I felt I was seeing the fruits of that persecution in the lives of the students I was teaching. All seemed to take it for granted that they would make sacrifices and, if necessary, suffer for their faith.

It was encouraging to work with such deeply committed Christians. Nevertheless that Christmas I experienced a certain heaviness of spirit. There was so much light-hearted banter about Carla's wedding – so much to remind me that when she left in six months time, I could be socializing alone. In my January prayer letter I again requested prayer for 'God's provision when Carla leaves.'

In retrospect it is interesting that I used the word 'provision' rather than 'companion', for provision rather than a companion is what I got. In February I went with Carla to N'Djamena for a short break. We both made the most of the opportunity to talk at length about the future. In the course of the conversation we touched on the subject of the little house that was being built at the Centre to accommodate occasional visitors – and suddenly a new thought hit me. 'Carla, I wonder whether that could be my house!'

No sooner were the words out of my mouth than we had a list of advantages. I'd have better accommodation, less travel, more contact with Moise and the students, more chance of an uninterrupted night's sleep.....

To my great delight the church and Mission leaders were all in favour of the idea and within a matter of weeks the decision was taken. God's provision, this time, came in the form of brick and mortar. That little house going up at the Centre was earmarked as my home.

Carla left in early July, after helping me move in. On my return to Ba Illi, having left her at the airport, I had difficulty opening the door of my house. Termites, I discovered, had gorged themselves on the doorframes. Still, it would have taken more than a load of hungry bugs to mar my satisfaction. I have always enjoyed home-making and the past few weeks with Carla had been enormous fun. We'd hung curtains and pictures, turned sheets into table covers and Carla insisted I should have her own beautiful bedspread for my bed. Now my nights were quiet. My new house did not leak. My bedroom window overlooked green fields – the pecking ground of an amazing variety of birds. Best of all I was close to African friends. Moise and Catherine lived within shouting distance and Moise made a point of popping in every day to say 'hello'. I also looked forward to getting to know the two new student families who'd moved in, ready for the new course starting in September.

Those summer months were a time of preparation and reflection. 8.00 am every morning found me at the makeshift table that served as my desk, where, if there were no visitors, I continued writing and studying until lunchtime. Although my lectures had been well received, I felt the need to alter them somewhat in the light of the particular needs and experience of African students. My talk on guidance, for example, reflected the individualism of Western Christianity. I needed to adjust it to fit the communal approach of African students, who readily equated God's guidance with the decisions of their Church leaders.

Seated at my 'desk', I prayed for the recent graduates. Some had had no idea where they were going until the actual day of their graduation. They had been prepared to accept, without question, the decisions of the mission leaders. And now they were out there: Valery and his wife amongst the Arabs, Jean and Affia with the Miltou people, Jacob amongst the little communities who live on the floating islands in Lake Chad. I had a sense of being removed from the action, in so far as I was not personally sharing Christ with these unreached peoples; at the same time I had a strong sense of connection through my input into the work of these national evangelists.

September came and the dawn of another academic year. If the highlights of my first year at the Centre had included seeing eight Christian couples of the highest spiritual calibre move out into active missionary service, one highlight of that second year was the opportunity to see the wonderful effect of such witness on a hitherto unreached tribe.

I had become aware of the Mbororo people very shortly after my arrival. In fact the two members of the tribe I'd spotted in the market had been amongst the many aspects of life I'd found so threatening in those early days. It was their fierceness that struck me, 'Who are those people?' I'd asked my companion nervously.

'They're nomads,' I was told. 'Their tribe is related to the Muslim Fulani of Nigeria. They aren't a poor people, but they are always on the move.'

Something about these tall, masterful yet socially unpopular people continued to draw my attention. I was particularly interested to learn that a handful of them had become Christians in recent months. The story of these conversions was linked with a man called Moussa – a Christian from the Tchaguine area, South of Ba Illi, who himself had been brought up a Muslim.

One afternoon, shortly after my move to the

Centre, I heard a knock at my door. My mouth dropped open when I discovered two imposing Mbororo on my doorstep. I was led to understand that one of them was a chief, and the other – the one with all the arrows – was Dogo, his bodyguard. 'We have come to greet you because we are Christians like you,' Chief Ngambo explained, proudly displaying the church membership cards carried by all Chadian believers.

Even more than the cards, the remarkably kind expressions on my visitors' faces gave me the confidence to invite them in. Over a cup of tea, the Chief consulted me about a problem. 'Soon it will be rainy season,' he said. 'We fear our cards will be destroyed in the rain and mud. Could you perhaps, give us something to protect them?'

I quickly produced two green, plastic cassette tape covers with exactly the right dimensions to keep church membership cards dry. 'Thank you! Thank you!' The Chief was overjoyed with this solution. If I had presented him with a couple of camels, he could not have been more pleased.

I too was thrilled with the encounter. Putting two and two together, I worked out that Chief Ngambo and Dogo must be amongst the handful of Mbororo whom Moussa had led to faith.

Then, a few months later, I had the opportunity to meet Moussa in person. By this stage the handful of Mbororo Christians had grown to around seventeen, and Moussa and his Church leaders felt he needed to learn more about cross-cultural evangelism. So he enrolled at the Centre for the 1995-96 academic year.

'When I come, the Mbororo will come too,' he promised.

And how right he was. Whenever the Mbororo were in the area, there was a constant stream of visitors to Moussa's door. What's more, in February the Chief decided that the whole Mbororo clan should congregate at the Centre for their annual four day feast.

From a spectator's point of view, it was fascinating to have a grandstand view of those celebrations – the elaborate preparations, the exquisitely embroidered costumes, the music, the dancing. I felt particularly privileged knowing that this wasn't in any way a show laid on for tourists. It was the genuine article – Mbororo culture having its traditional annual fling. Still, this was a feast with a difference, for the Chief had brought his people to the Centre with the expressed desire that on Sunday morning they should all hear the word of God.

A few weeks later, after a long conversation with church elders, the Chief, Dogo and another Mbororo Christian called Abakhar were baptised. This deeply moving event took place in the river which flowed past the Centre.

Possibly for the first time in his adult life, the Chief publicly removed his turban and walked into the water with the other two men. It took great humility, but the spiritual joy of all three was clearly apparent.

'You must come and visit us,' the Chief said to me on a number of occasions after that. 'Yes. I will,' I'd replied each time. But for over twelve months my schedule kept ruling out the possibility of such an expedition. 'We'll soon be moving,' the Chief informed me one day when I met him at Moussa's house. I was near the end of my four year term in Chad by this stage, and realized this could be my last chance to make something I'd promised come true.

'Could I get my car through the bush to your camp?' I inquired.

My prospective host beamed. 'There is a road and it will take the feet of an ox-cart. It will surely take the feet of your car.'

'All right then.' I turned to Moussa. 'Let's go!'

The road which the Chief had spoken of turned out to be little more than a glorified track. Moussa and I ended up with Mbororo youths marching ahead of us, cutting back the undergrowth to let us through. Eventually we drove into a clearing surrounded by a semi-circle of thorn hedges.

The camp seemed relatively deserted when

we arrived, but within minutes news of our coming had spread. Chief Ngambo made us welcome and people started to appear from all directions. An enormous sheep was slaughtered and roasted over a hole in the ground. As the guest of honour, I was presented with the choicest cuts – a steaming bowl of entrails. My sharp intake of breath was not lost on the Chief. 'Is there something wrong? Does God not allow us to eat entrails?' he inquired.

That simple question brought home to me the extent to which this brother, who could not read the Bible for himself, was looking to the example of other believers to discover how to live the Christian life. 'Entrails are fine,' I assured him, tucking into the gritty, leathery fare with what I hoped was some semblance of relish.

I was conscious meanwhile of a certain amount of hacking going on in the undergrowth behind my back. On turning round, I discovered that the women of the tribe were busy making up my bed.

Throughout the night more and more Mbororo continued to arrive. I slept fitfully on a table-high tree platform covered with a mat made from bark. The women had retired to similar platforms, while their menfolk simply bedded down in holes in the sand. 'If only my family could see me now!' I thought as I lay there surrounded by snoring Mbororo men.

But my most unforgettable experience came next morning when everyone gathered to hear the word of God. Without doubt there had been a move of the Spirit amongst these people. During the time I'd spent in Chad, the first handful of converts had become a group of almost one hundred believers. That day, as Moussa spoke God's truth to them, the clearing was packed. I sat there watching this Chadian brother speak lovingly and effectively to those of another culture than his own, and it was a moment of profound fulfilment.

Four years earlier I had come to this country with two major questions. The first had been a personal question, springing from the emotional baggage I'd carried with me from Namibia. Could I cope with this new assignment? I now knew that, by the grace of God, the answer to that question was 'yes'. At times, during the four years, it had been a close-run thing. I'd cried out in my weakness to colleagues in Chad and friends at home, but there had been no repetition of the dark agonies of the past. I knew when the time came I would leave the country with a sense of victory, not defeat.

The second question related to the work I'd come to do. I'd been involved in sharing a body of knowledge and experience with the indigenous Church. The question was would this actually help them in their efforts to spread the gospel in Chad? Again, I now knew the answer was 'yes'. I had seen students go out from the Missionary Centre and translate theory into practice. They were being culturally sensitive in their witness, winning members of people-groups other than their own for Christ.

Watching Moussa preach to that Mbororo congregation – a people who, a few years earlier, had known nothing of the Christian faith – I had the sense that this was what it was all about. Here was a man on the cutting edge of mission – and the Missionary Centre had helped equip him for the task. So I savoured that moment, sitting there in the heart of the African bush. Chad had been my toughest assignment, but also my best. God had given me the strength to climb my dream-wall; and this was the view from the top.

EPILOGUE
October 1999

When writing the prologue to this book, I referred to a Bible story – John's record of the feeding of the five thousand. I mentioned how God had spoken to me through the gathering up of the scraps of bread and fish at the end of the meal; how I felt he was encouraging me to share some of the lessons I had learnt over the past thirty-five years.

Today, as I complete this sharing process, it is with another biblical image in mind – the image of the psalmist, with God's help, scaling a wall (Psalm 18:29). I look back over the years and see many walls along the way – the wall of parental opposition, the wall of shattered dreams, the wall of failure, the wall of fear. I recall times when those walls loomed huge and unyielding and the temptation was to alter my course in search of an easier path.

Even as I write I'm conscious of a fresh wall on my personal journey. At the end of this month, after just over a year on home assignment, I am due to return to Chad. One of my main tasks this time will be to help organize and take part in a refresher course for former students at the Missionary Centre.

It would be reasonable to imagine that someone who has already spent four years in Chad, teaching a variety of courses, should be able to take this more limited assignment in her stride. The truth is, I feel thoroughly daunted at the thought of what lies ahead. Of course I'm longing to see Chadian friends and colleagues again. But I know my physical and spiritual stamina is about to be tested – tested to the limits.

And yet I also know that of all the lessons I've learnt, the most important is this: his strength is made perfect in weakness (2 Cor. 12:9). God is able to deal with the walls. He won't let anything block us in our progress along the path of his choosing. He may not always miraculously knock down the walls, but he does enable us to climb them, and so to say: 'My feet have closely followed his steps; I have kept to his way without turning aside' (Job 23:11).

Maybe, like me, you are facing a wall – a challenge or a set of circumstances that threatens to overwhelm you. I pray that if this book does one thing, it will encourage you to keep going. We are not alone. Our loving God has gone before us, and at the same time as we mount the difficulties, he is there at our backs; there to catch us when we fall, there to steady us as we climb, there to shoulder our every burden and gently lift us to new heights.